God, the Poet and the Devil

For Rose and Tony

God, the Poet and the Devil

Robert Burns and Religion

DONALD SMITH

SAINT ANDREW PRESS
Edinburgh

First published in 2008 by
SAINT ANDREW PRESS
121 George Street
Edinburgh EH2 4YN

ISBN 978 0 7152 0876 2

British Library Cataloguing in Publication Data
A catalogue record for this book is available from the British Library

Typeset by Waverley Typesetters, Fakenham
Manufactured in Great Britain by MPG Books, Bodmin

Contents

List of Illustrations
in Plate Section

Acknowledgements

I would like to thank my teachers, particularly Professor John MacQueen formerly Director of the School of Scottish Studies at the University of Edinburgh, and the late Professor Alec Cheyne. I would also like to thank my fellow storytellers and my colleagues on the Literature Forum of Scotland who have provided constant stimulus and friendship. Finally, I am indebted to Marjory Carnegie for her indomitable secretarial support.

Introduction

Thirty years ago Professor Alec Cheyne of New College set me thinking about the subject of Robert Burns and religion. His point was twofold. Without understanding Christianity in late eighteenth-century Scotland, Burns is an enigma. But equally, the poetry of Burns provides penetrating insights into religious life in Scotland and religion in general.

My professional life has been on that cusp of religion and culture ever since, so the 250th anniversary of the birth of Burns is an ideal opportunity to finally pull together these thoughts.

This book can also be read as a companion piece to my novel *Between Ourselves* which looks at the subjective and, at times, corrosive aspects of the poet's sense of himself, of others, of the divine and of the dark. In these pages, however, speculation is restrained in favour of our rich knowledge of the human being, his relationships and his works. The picture that emerges is of a complex man who lived life to the full and defined himself and his art through, and often against, the Christianity of his time.

My aim here is broadly thematic, and tailored for the general reader. A succession of fine scholars have provided vital background including most recently Professor Liam

McIlvanney and the Rev. J. Walter McGinty, whose *Robert Burns and Religion* can be heartily recommended to all those who would like to explore Burns's context more fully. The best account of the poems and songs bearing on religion is still Thomas Crawford's, in his classic *Burns: A Study of the Poems and Songs*. A short bibliography of the key books used in this study is provided at the end of the text.

I hope very much that the 250th anniversary will provide a real opportunity to come to grips with the full stature of Robert Burns as an artist and as a human being.

Dr Donald Smith
The Scottish Storytelling Centre

Chapter One

Clearing the Ground

Commentary on the theme of Robert Burns and religion is bedevilled by use of terms such as 'Calvinist', 'Presbyterian' and 'Auld Licht versus New Licht'. Often these are used inaccurately and even more often pejoratively, as if the mere word 'Calvinist' or 'Presbyterian' obviously denoted something nay-saying and repressive. Understanding Burns in context requires a more careful and less technical or even prejudicial vocabulary.

From the Scottish Reformation of 1560, Protestantism gradually became the dominant form of Christianity in Scotland. Roman Catholicism, Episcopalianism and independent or dissenting churches all, to some degree, exerted an influence on Scottish life but the institutions of religion – parish kirks, universities and schools – were the responsibility of the national Church and the source of its connection with society as a whole.

To describe this national Church as presbyterian is not entirely accurate. John Calvin had laid down in Geneva the blueprint for a godly church and society in which the practice of (according to Calvin) 'Biblical' forms of Church government were restored, and the civil powers were required to heed the teaching of the reformed faith and

1

impose its vision of social order and personal morality. This blueprint was developed by John Knox and colleagues, and later by Andrew Melville, but it was never fully applied in Scotland.

In one vital particular, Scotland's national Church had continued in the eighteenth century to fall short of the Calvinist and Presbyterian ideals. Ministers were not, except for a brief seventeenth-century period, 'called' or 'elected' by the people of God in congregations, but appointed by landowners and magistrates.

Moreover, the Church never secured the resources needed to apply the reformed vision of universal education and social care. Most of the considerable resources of the medieval Catholic Church went into the coffers of landowners and, to a lesser extent, Burgh Councils. The reformed kirk could barely scrape sufficient cash to pay an educated ministry.

Finally, Calvinist doctrines were embodied in the Scots Confession approved by Parliament in 1560 and the Westminster Confession of 1647. This teaching emphasised the sole authority of the Bible in matters religious, the supremacy of Christ in Church and State, and the degradation of human nature through the Fall, with a consequent need for divine salvation to avert damnation to Hell. Some versions of Calvinism went further in emphasising that, due to God's foreknowledge, human beings were predestined to salvation or damnation but could not themselves know for certain to which end they were heading.

In some regards, these doctrines continued medieval emphases but in others they broke decisively with the past. By denying the role of the Church in providing a pathway to Heaven rather than Hell the new teaching put great pressure on the individual to examine their metaphysical and moral state. The believer became an instrument of judgement as well as an evangel of salvation 'through Jesus Christ'. However, despite the best efforts of preachers and catechists across the generations, it is questionable whether such beliefs were ever held or practised in a pure form by a majority of Scotland's population. Folk religion continued inside and outside the kirks and many educated Scots remained resistant to doctrines of 'human corruption', retaining a belief in the power of human will and action to make a positive difference.

By Burns's own time, the hold of traditional Calvinism had slackened as economic and social changes impacted on church and community. But this was not a clear-cut opposition between old and new, progressive and reactionary. For one thing, the religion which had driven the seventeenth-century Covenanters (not least in Ayrshire) combined political radicalism with religious conservativism. By contrast, many of the so-called 'enlightenment' progressives or moderates were politically conservative, deploying religion as a means of hierarchical influence to underpin social order while driving forward economic change.

During Burns's lifetime, traditional Calvinist or (perhaps more correctly) Puritan piety was transposing into a new dynamic Evangelical movement which was to transform Scottish society in the nineteenth century. While attacking the Puritans, Burns's own writing espouses a religion of the heart which is in harmony with emergent evangelical emphases. At the same time, Burns adopts an intellectual stance in line with the 'religion of sense and reason', promoted by the Enlightenment luminaries such as William Robertson, Hugh Blair and Dugald Stewart. It is perhaps significant that Burns embraces much of these men's thinking, while regarding some of them as arrant snobs disconnected from the wider Scottish community.

In short, the 'progressive' and 'reactionary' labels need to be rethought and challenged by looking at what Burns actually wrote and felt. The picture that emerges is more interesting than the labels and perhaps more relevant to the position of religion in the contemporary world. If at points Burns may seem to hold contradictory attitudes together it is because his times were complex and subject to rapid change.

There are three distinct periods to Robert Burns's life. His formation in Ayrshire, his brief but critical period in the capital city and on tour, and his short-lived maturity in Dumfriesshire. However, there is no evidence of major shifts in Burns's outlook on religion after his teenage years. His attitudes were early formed and remarkably persistent. That is why, although this book draws on biographical and autobiographical sources, it is structured around key themes.

Chapter Two

Education

Robert Burns was born in 1759 as the child of a tenant farmer. The Burns family, or Burnes as it was then spelt, were not peasants but they were entirely dependent for their living on a succession of small farms, none of which benefited from prime land or the agricultural improvements being applied by estate managers.

Robert's mother, Agnes Burnes, was born Agnes Brown and came from typical Ayrshire farming stock. Agnes was marked by strong religious faith and her attachment to local language and culture. She rejected an earlier longstanding fiancé, in favour of the older and more serious William Burnes, when the younger man formed a sexual liaison behind her back. Casual sexual relationships in and out of wedlock were common in agricultural communities and, if kirk session records are to be believed, were more prevalent in Ayrshire in the eighteenth century than they had been in the pious seventeenth.

Significantly, Agnes could not write even her name and is unlikely to have been literate in the modern sense but she was a singer and always ready to entertain and instruct her children. Her role seems always to have been as 'woman of the house' and she sustained this contribution as mother,

mother-in-law and grandmother into a ripe old age. Burns's loyalty to his mother and his sense of responsibility to the household of his brother Gilbert, in which she lived out her days, continued to his own death. Like Burns's own wife Jean Armour, Agnes Brown also undertook the upbringing of Robert's children from his extramarital relationships.

Robert's father, William Burnes, by contrast was not a typical Ayrshire farmer. His family had been settled for many generations in the Mearns until economic troubles drove William south as a young man. The Burnes had been tenants and sometimes retainers of the aristocratic Keiths, the Earls Marischal of Scotland, and it was a deeply held belief of Robert's that his family had suffered for their loyalty to the Keiths and to the Jacobite cause in the 1715 rising.

There is no definite evidence for this but it is clear that the Burnes family held their land as single tenants in direct relationship to the Earls. It is also certain that the penalties inflicted on the Jacobite Keiths began a trend of increasing economic difficulties for their tenants and retainers. This, combined with the challenges of farming marginal land in the face of larger-scale improved units, drove the Burnes family off the land, some to poverty and some in due course to town-based prosperity.

William Burnes found work in Edinburgh as a gardener helping lay out Hope Park near the Meadows and then moved to Alloway as an estate gardener. It is, however, clear throughout that William wanted his own household independence which was the family tradition. He built his cottage in Alloway and began to develop a market garden. Then, as opportunity arose, he took a lease on a farm at Mount Oliphant, becoming master of his own house.

Robert later interpreted this move as a desire on his father's part to keep the family together, rather than disperse his children as farm servants in other households as was customary with the labouring class. Those who label 'A Cottar's Saturday Night' as 'sentimental' should note Robert's profound gratitude for his family upbringing. Life as a farm servant would have deprived the talented youngster of many vital opportunities as well as emotional support. William Burnes was passionately devoted to the allied causes of education and self improvement – ideals which he vigorously instilled in his growing sons. Burnes's religious devotion and intellectual achievement went together since serious study was the means by which the nature and purposes of God and his creation could become better known. Knowledge and morality, in his view, reinforced each other and increased an individual's contribution to the wellbeing of the wider community.

This determination is the more remarkable because the Burnes family had little access to conventional schooling to back it up. Despite the ambition of the Reformers in 1560 to have a school in every parish, and a 1696 Education Act that sought to implement the ideal, the nearest parish school was in Ayr. To counteract this, William and some fellow farmers clubbed together to employ a schoolteacher for their families. This arrangement which lasted for less than two years, along with short periods in Ayr and Irvine, was Robert Burns's only experience of formal education.

Moreover, William's ambitions for Robert and Gilbert were severely restricted by the economic hardships of small-scale farming. As children, the boys were trained up to be farm workers, and from Robert's early teens both brothers were putting in a full day's work as ploughmen. There was no alternative since finances simply could not stretch to hired labour. The pressures of such hard physical labour on a growing boy may account for some of Robert's later health problems. They certainly shaped his sense of fairness and injustice as, bit by bit, he saw his father broken by the system.

It would be wrong, however, to place too much emphasis on Robert's lack of formal schooling because he was brought up from the start to seize every opportunity for learning that both his family and the wider community provided. The fact that he seized these avidly was to be decisive in his formation as both a human being and an artist.

Community tradition remained an important medium of education in eighteenth-century rural Ayrshire. Often this was passed on through songs, oral stories and family history, but the centres of literate culture (including churches, schools, local libraries and clubs, landed households and Masonic lodges) were also interested in traditional culture. Robert's vivid account of his mother's cousin Betty Davidson's supernatural folk tales at the family hearth has rather deflected attention from the wider role of tradition in educating the poet.

'The Vision' is a very early and very ambitious poem of Burns, published in the *Kilmarnock Edition* of his works. It is a self-consciously literary effort, borrowing elements of tone and structure from MacPherson's Ossian but 'The Vision' is firmly rooted in the poet's own rural landscape and way of life.

The Sun had clos'd the winter-day,	
The Curlers quat their roaring play,	left
And hunger'd maukin taen her way,	hare
To kail-yards green,	
While faithless snaws ilk step betray	each
Whare she has been.	
The Thresher's weary flingin-tree,	flail
The lee-lang day had tired me;	
And when the Day had clos'd his e'e	
Far i' the West,	
Ben i' the spence, right pensivelie,	parlour
I gaed to rest.	
There, lanely by the ingle-cheek,	
I sat and ey'd the spewing reek,	smoke
That fill'd, wi hoast-provoking smeek,	cough / fumes
The auld clay biggin;	
An' heard the restless rattons squeak	
About the riggin.[1]	rafters

The exhausted farmer is then visited at his own winter fireside by Coila, a legendary muse or spirit of place, who has given her name to Kyle, Burns's homeland. Courtesy of Coila, the farmer poet proceeds to display a detailed knowledge

[1] W. E. Henley (ed.), *The Complete Writings of Robert Burns* (London: The Waverley Book Co., 1927), Vol. I, pp. 209–10.

of the region's traditional history, its earldoms and landed families, and the character of its landscape, all of which are celebrated in song and story. In many ways, 'The Vision' is an ambivalent poem as Burns seems to be evoking a role – that of a traditional bard strumming his lyre in honour of the local establishment – which he has no intention of following. Nonetheless, the poem demonstrates the extent to which Burns had absorbed rich regional and patriotic traditions.

Another side of the poet's community learning is evident in his early observations of rural life such as 'Hallowe'en'. Descriptive and humorous, as opposed to satiric, 'Hallowe'en' presents a detailed picture of rural life and traditions in very rich and dense Scots:

The auld Guidwife's weel-hoordet nits   well-hoarded nuts
  Are round an' round divided,
An' monie lads' an' lasses' fates
  Are there that night decided:
Some kindle couthie, side by side,   friendly
  An' burn thegither trimly
Some start awa wi' saucy pride,
  An' jump out-owre the chimlie
   Fu' high that night.[2]

The metrical form of 'Hallowe'en' draws on a tradition of Lowland Scots poems of folk festivity. But Burns is concerned to give people a full and comprehensible picture by providing his own notes. So on the above stanza he comments:

[2] Ibid., Vol. I, pp. 228–9.

Burning the nuts is a favourite charm. They name the lad and lass to each particular nut as they lay them in the fire and, accordingly as they burn quietly together, or start from beside one another, the course and issue of the courtship will be.

Other forms of Hallowe'en divination are carefully detailed:

This charm must likewise be performed unperceived and alone. You go to the barn and open both doors, taking them off the hinges if possible; for there is danger that the being that is about to appear may shut the doors and do you some mischief. Then take that instrument used in winnowing the corn, which in our country-dialect we call a 'wecht', and go through all the attitudes of letting down corn against the wind. Repeat it three times and, the third time, an apparition will pass through the barn, in at the windy door and out at the other, having both the figure in question and the appearance of retinue, marking the employment or station in life.

Take an opportunity of going unnoticed to a 'bear-stack' [stack of bere or bigg, a kind of barley] and fathom it three times round. The last fathom of the last time you will catch in your arms the appearance of your future conjugal yoke-fellow.

Alongside these details of popular folk belief are explanations of historical references and of food and drink:

Saucers, with butter instead of milk, to them, is always the Hallowe'en supper.

The 'to them' is revealing since Burns the poet is aiming to communicate beyond this traditional rural culture and therefore needs to explain it to educated outsiders. Nonetheless, 'Hallowe'en' richly demonstrates the extent to which Robert participated in the culture of his community, absorbed and understood it outwith formal education. In this, he was not a lone alienated figure but part of a vigorously self-reflecting and proud culture.

The perspective of an insider communicating beyond his immediate context is central to many of the early works. These include 'The Auld Farmer's New-Year Morning Salutation to His Auld Mare, Maggy', 'Scotch Drink', 'Death and Doctor Hornbook', 'To A Louse' and 'A Mauchline Wedding'. The stance of the writer is humorous but sympathetic and redolent of a social education that nurtured Robert's innate gifts far beyond any 'book learning'. Burns is supremely a poet of human relations and of what psychologists now call social intelligence.

However, it is also important to move on to say that, in Robert's upbringing, book learning was not restricted to schooling. At home, William Burnes provided a small but treasured collection of theological and historical works. He was also a subscriber to the Ayr library and, through his friendship with the young teacher John Murdoch and his contacts, was able to give Robert access to a widening circle of literature.

The first book to which Robert was directed at home was the Bible which he read avidly and to good purpose. Both his poems and his letters are saturated with Biblical references and metaphors. Although scriptural texts were central to family worship and to church services, William encouraged his son to read critically and appreciatively, not by rote or in awe of standard clerical instruction. Among the volumes which William Burnes purchased in sections by subscription was John Stackhouse's *History of the Bible* which set the scriptural text in its wider historical context. This approach to Biblical exegesis became central to the more theologically liberal interpretations, in contrast to the method of accumulating 'proof texts' which was favoured by the Puritan divines, including the authors of the Westminster Confession.

What was the source of William Burnes's independent thinking and his determination to have his sons think for themselves? It has been suggested that the Burnes family may have had Episcopalian leanings but there is no evidence for this other than continuing Episcopal sympathies in the Mearns. And anyway, Scottish Episcopalianism in the seventeenth and early eighteenth centuries was very close to the Presbyterians in style of worship and theological doctrine. The big difference was in church government, and bishops did not preach radical dissent. The shaping of William Burnes and of his son Robert lies in Presbyterianism itself. Those whose experience of the Presbyterian churches lies in the twentieth century often characterise the tradition as conformist and socially conservative. It would, however, be a major error to read this state of affairs back into the eighteenth century when Presbyterianism was a hotbed of dispute and dissent.

In the seventeenth century, the main fault line had been between Episcopalian and Presbyterian traditions and their respective relationships to the State. Much storm and fury, and not a few lives, had been expended over this argument. The accession of William and Mary in 1688–9 put Presbyterianism in pole position in Scotland, but merely set the scene for a new set of disputes.

First of all the Covenanters, who were strong in the south-west of Scotland, refused to accept the Presbyterian settlement because it did not explicitly endorse the National Covenant (1638) and the Solemn League and Covenant (1643). Effectively, these documents were much too politically radical for the new establishment of Kirk and State, not least on issues of royal government, so the Covenanters stayed out to become later the Reformed Presbyterian tradition.

The Treaty of Union between England and Scotland of 1707 appeared in black and white to confirm the Williamite Settlement but, five years later in 1712, the House of Lords in the Parliament of the new United Kingdom imposed 'lay patronage' on Scotland, i.e. appointment of ministers by landed proprietors. This led in due course to a series of secessions from the Church of Scotland through the eighteenth century.

The Secessionists themselves later split on another issue of Church–State relationships, the 'Burger Oath', and it was out of this split that the 'Auld Licht / New Licht' distinction arose. In fact, both sides in this argument were theologically conservative while varying in their degree of radical dissent from the exercise of civil power over the Church. A more theologically driven movement for change was provided in 1761 by the Relief Secession which sought a broader, more inclusive style of Presbyterianism than the Calvinist Puritans, while agreeing with them on opposing lay patronage!

The impulse across all these Presbyterian groupings was towards critical debate. No minister was safe from a detailed examination of his views followed by disagreements, arguments and sometimes outright revolt. Moreover, in general, class distinction was also at work. The upper classes tended to support the Presbyterian establishment whose ministers they appointed, while weavers, artisans and townspeople were active dissenters. The emergent middle classes could split in both directions depending on local circumstances. These divisions were vigorously pursued within, as well as between, the different churches and the arguments were often fiercest within the Church of Scotland.

This digression into church history is not intended to bewilder with splits and divisions, but to highlight the key principle of dissent which is very relevant to William Burnes. He fostered and practised a combination of critical thinking with deep piety. He 'sat', as the saying went, under ministers (such as Dr William Dalrymple at the Auld Kirk of Ayr) who were noted for their piety, civic virtue and advanced thinking. Nothing was more significant in this Presbyterian environment than one's choice of minister.

In addition, Burnes left nothing to chance in the education of his own sons into a lively Protestant inheritance of sincere piety, devotion to virtue and rational thought. At William's request and with his assistance, John Murdoch, the dominie who shared William's principles, prepared for Robert and Gilbert *A Manual of Religious Belief in the Form of a Dialogue*

Between Father and Son. Such manuals were a traditional part of Presbyterian and Puritan piety, ensuring that home, church and school were united by instilling religion in the young. What, though, is significant about the Burnes manual was its difference from the traditional models and its one-off 'bespoke quality'.

The standard method of religious instruction in the eighteenth as in the seventeenth century was the Catechism, a series of questions and answers to be learned by rote. A series of such Catechisms were produced, but the dominant one in Robert's youth was *The Shorter Catechism* prepared by the Westminster Assembly in 1648 along with its Confession, and backed up by a series of scriptural texts or 'proofs'.

The emphasis of the Catechism is squarely on what the child ought in due course to know, rather than on a young person's capacity or understanding. It is also highly theoretical and abstract, depending more on scholastic Calvinist theology than on an inner quickening of spiritual experience. A flavour is in order, since the tone and rhythms of *The Shorter Catechism* penetrated deeply into the Scottish psyche.

17. Q: Into what state did the fall bring mankind?
    A: The fall brought mankind into a state of sin and misery

18. Q: Wherein consists the sinfulness of that state into which man fell?
    A: The sinfulness of that state into which man fell, consists in the guilt of Adam's first sin, the want of

original righteousness, and the corruption of his whole nature, which is commonly called original sin; together with all actual transgressions which proceed from it.

19. Q: What is the misery of that state into which man fell?

A: All mankind by their fall lost communion with God, are under his wrath and curse, and so made liable to all miseries in this life, to death itself, and to the pains of hell for ever.

20. Q: Did God leave all mankind to perish in the state of sin and misery?

A: God having, out of his mere good pleasure, from all eternity, elected some to everlasting life, did enter into a covenant of grace, to deliver them out of the estate of sin and misery, and to bring them into a state of salvation by a Redeemer.[3]

Redemption or salvation in Christ is a stern and grievous process in the Catechism, not least for the Saviour (Christ) whose 'humiliation consisted on His being born, and that in a low condition, made under the law, undergoing the miseries of this life, the wrath of God, and the cursed death of the Cross'. Fortunately, the Resurrection of Christ was the work of divine providence and, like the Fall, this too becomes part of the inheritance of humanity subject to 'effectual calling'.

31. Q: What is effectual calling?

A: Effectual calling is the work of God's Spirit, whereby, convincing us of our sin and misery, enlightening our

[3] Thomas F. Torrance (ed.), *The School of Faith* (London: James Clarke & Co., 1959), p. 265.

> minds in the knowledge of Christ, and renewing our
> wills, he doth persuade and enable us to embrace
> Jesus Christ, freely offered to us in the gospel.[4]

The only alternative to 'effectual calling' is perpetual damnation to the torments of Hell.

Notable in all this is its remorselessly impersonal tone. The Catechist seems the mouthpiece of a God who demands and instructs, condemns and reproves with impartial logic and an almost total absence of emotion. Compare this model of instruction with William Burnes's *Dialogue* with his sons. The *Manual* which Murdoch prepared is based on a loving partnership between parent and child which encourages questioning and enquiry. There is no lack of heavy-duty theology, but the tone is genuinely educative and encouraging.[5]

The Burnes *Manual* places emphasis on the experience of religion and, above all, a struggle between goodness and love on the one hand and the 'lower' nature of 'animal instincts' on the other. Sin is still very much to the fore but the overall aim is not the destruction of the animal self but its reconciliation resulting in 'true enjoyment' of instinct. The purpose of religion is to restore the harmony of the created order as God intended. This will make humanity fit for Christ's spiritual kingdom but also restore 'pleasure and

---

[4] Ibid., Vol. I, pp. 266–7.
[5] *The Manual of Religious Belief in the Form of a Dialogue Between Father and Son* existed in manuscript form but was published in Robert Chambers (ed.), *The Life and Works of Robert Burns*, as revised by William Wallace (Edinburgh and London: W. & R. Chambers, 1896), Vol. I, pp. 455ff.

joy'. Spiritual life is not presented in the *Manual* as a grievous struggle but as a quest for peace of mind and the calming of 'irregular passions'. Ultimately this will be achieved by bringing 'all our interests under the care of our Heavenly Father'. The point of the Bible is not to provide an armoury of 'proof' texts but a commentary on 'a Christian or holy life'. The Gospels are much quoted and, in particular, the Sermon on the Mount.

It is hard to overestimate the significance of the *Manual* due both to its contemporary distinctiveness and to its clear influence on Burns's own thinking and feelings. Above all the *Manual* is an expression of the father–son relationship as embodied in William Burnes's own life and example. The sense of a benevolent Father and Creator remained, for Robert, the enduring emotional and intellectual core of religion throughout his life, whatever the adolescent ups and downs of his own family experience. To these themes we shall return in later chapters.

Two dominant images emerge from Robert Burns's formative teenage years. One is the voracious reader later described by David Sillars, a close friend of the poet as he emerged into adulthood. On walks, and even at meals, Burns had a book in hand. Any interruption in the regime of farm labour was an excuse to imbibe more knowledge and experience. According to Sillars, the younger Burns read deeply in theology but increasingly widened his tastes on a literary diet. Getting his hands on books, first through his father's influence and later on his own account through reading clubs like the Tarbolton Bachelors Club, was essential to feeding this keen hunger.

The other image is the one that Burns himself penned in 'The Cotter's Saturday Night'. The family gathers by the hearth of a humble cottage or farmhouse:

> *With joy unfeign'd, brothers and sisters meet,*
> *And each for other's welfare kindly spiers:*   enquirers
> *The social hours, swift-wing'd, unnotic'd fleet;*
> *Each tells the uncos that he sees or hears.*   news
> *The parents partial eye their hopeful years;*
> *Anticipation forward points the view;*
> *The Mother, wi' her needle and her sheers,*
> *Gars auld claes look amaist as weel's the new;*[6]   almost

The daughter's suitor comes calling and Burns is led into some rather strained apostrophising to 'O happy love'. But the poem moves on smoothly to the 'simple board' and then to the focus of the poem – family prayers.

> *The cheerfu' supper done, wi' serious face,*
> *They, round the ingle, form a circle wide;*
> *The Sire turns o'er wi' patriarchal grace;*
> *The big ha'-Bible, ance his father's pride.*   hall Bible
> *His bonnet rev'rently is laid aside,*
> *His lyart haffets wearing thin and bare;*   grey locks
> *Those strains that once did sweet in Zion glide,*
> *He wales a portion with judicious care;*   selects
> *'And let us worship God!' he says, with solemn air.*[7]

---

[6] Henley, Vol. II, p. 248.
[7] Ibid., Vol. I, p. 251.

Like the social descriptions, this has the authenticity of direct observation. If William Burnes, however, is the visual centre of the scene, it is Robert Burns's perspective which informs its Biblical commentary.

The priest-like Father reads the sacred page,
  How Abram was the Friend of God on high;
Or, Moses bade eternal warfare wage
  With Amalek's ungracious progeny;
Or, how the royal Bard did groaning lye
  Beneath the stroke of Heaven's avenging ire;
Or Job's pathetic plaint, and wailing cry;
  Or rapt Isaiah's wild, seraphic fire;
Or other Holy Seers that tune the sacred lyre.

Perhaps the Christian Volume is the theme:
  How guiltless blood for guilty man was shed;
How He, who bore in Heaven the second name,
  Had not on Earth whereon to lay His head;
How His first followers and servants sped;
  The Precepts sage they wrote to many a land:
How he, who lone in Patmos banished,
  Saw in the sun a mighty angel stand,
And heard great Bab'lon's doom pronounc'd by Heaven's
  command.[8]

The culmination of the poem follows in the contrast between the familial socially grounded experience of religion in the

[8] Ibid., Vol. I, pp. 252–3.

cottage and the institutional powerplay of ecclestiastical pride of all varieties.

Then kneeling down to Heaven's Eternal King
    The saint, the father and the husband prays:
Hope 'springs exulting on triumphant wing',
    That thus they all shall meet on future days
There ever bask in uncreated rays,
    No more to sigh or shed the bitter tear,
Together hymning their Creator's praise,
    In such society, yet still more dear;
While circling Time moves round in an eternal sphere.

Compared with this how poor religion's pride,
    In all the pomp of method and of art;
When men display to congregations wide
    Devotions' ev'ry grace, except the heart!
The power, incens'd, the pageant will desert,
    The pompous strain, the sacerdotal stole;
But haply, in some cottage far apart,
    May hear, well-pleas'd, the language of the soul,
And in His Book of Life the inmates poor enrol.[9]

The closing stanzas of 'The Cotter's Saturday Night' are the poem's most famous, prefaced by 'From scenes like these, old Scotia's grandeur springs', but the rhetoric of the peroration is actually unnecessary and much abused by later proponents of 'Scottish national virtue'. The telling images of the poem are not a rhetorical statement, because they directly express

[9] Ibid., Vol. I, pp. 253–4.

a devotion which makes no public or worldly claims to attention.

'The Cotter's Saturday Night' has been heavily criticised for its English tone and diction, its sentimentality and its, at points, overblown rhetoric. However, it is a genuinely religious poem based on Burns's own family life and, often, the criticisms seem to stem from its later use to promote conventional piety and cloying patriotism rather than the work itself. The tone is carefully balanced and sustained in the elegiac mode of eighteenth-century English literature. The emotional core, however, is undoubtedly a retrospective tribute to the sincere Christianity of William Burnes. The man who taught his son the religion of the *Manual* also lived his creed. After his father's death in 1784, Robert penned a heartfelt tribute to the man who, more than any other, had shaped his outlook and values.

O ye whose cheek the tear of pity stains
Draw near with pious rev'rence, and attend!
Here lie the loving Husband's dear remains,
The tender Father, and the gen'rous Friend.

The pitying Heart that felt for human Woe,
The dauntless heart that fear'd no human Pride;
The Friend of Man, to vice alone a foe;
For 'ev'n his failings lean'd to Virtue's side'.[10]

These words are engraved on the tombstone in Alloway Kirkyard.

---

[10] Ibid., Vol. I, p. 62.

Chapter Three

Poetry

When Robert Burns's first book, the *Kilmarnock Edition* of his poems, was published in 1786 it appeared as if the author had sprung into life a fully formed poet. Of course, Burns was already 27 years old and had behind him several years of tentative experiment and his local celebrity status. As a 'samizdat' poet his works were copied, handed round and recited, often by the sociable Burns himself. Nom de plumes such as 'Rab Rhymer' or 'Ruisseaux' (French for 'burns') fooled no-one, friend or enemy.

This is partly the result of brilliant editing. Assisted (or was it restrained?) by his patron and friend Gavin Hamilton and his own brother Gilbert, Robert contrived to present a poetic persona of tremendous assurance and chutzpah. This was done by limiting Burns's more melancholic strains, excluding earlier works with a conventional tendency and, of course, discarding or editing poems which were directly offensive to named local individuals or the Church. Only at the close of the collection, with the tribute to his dead father and the rueful 'A Bard's Epitaph', did the confident mask seem to slip. The careful focusing of the *Kilmarnock Edition*, which lead to its successful marketing and, finally, critical acclaim demonstrates how far Robert Burns was from the stereotype of a naïve rustic versifier.

Behind the finished product of 1786 is a progressive search for understanding of self, society and world. Experiences of family, church, community and reading all contributed to this process but the engine was a very Protestant desire to place soul and self in a conscious relationship with the 'sum of things'. In this, Robert is his father's son; but he was to go much further by coalescing his search for understanding with a poetic vocation. Underlying all Burns's modes from rustic bard to song maker, correspondent in verse, and social commentator, is the poet as an enlightened perceiver and maker of truth.

Fragments of Burns's early religious verse appear in the *Kilmarnock Edition* and as fillers in the Edinburgh editions of his poems. These include a very creditable 'Paraphrase of the First Psalm':

The man, in life wherever plac'd,
    Hath happiness in store,
Who walks not in the wicked's way,
    Nor learns their guilty lore;

Nor from the seat of Scornful Pride
    Casts forth his eyes abroad,
But with humility and awe
    Still walks before his God.

That Man shall flourish like the trees
    Which by the streamlets grow:

The fruitful top is spread on high,
    And firm the root below.[1]

The paraphrase was probably written in 1781–2 and there is evidence that, at this time, Burns's language for truth was still primarily theological. The period also coincides with Robert's unsuccessful attempts to branch out on his own in Irvine. From there he wrote to his father:

My principal, and indeed my only pleasurable employment is looking backwards and forwards in a moral and religious way. I am quite transported at the thought that ere long, perhaps very soon, I shall bid an eternal adieu to all the pains, and uneasiness and disquietudes of this weary life: for I assure you I am heartily tired of it, and, if I do not very much much deceive myself I could contentedly and gladly resign it

The Soul uneasy and confin'd from home,
Rests and expatiates in a life to come.

[Pope]

It is for this reason I am more pleased with the 15th, 16th and 17th verses of the 7th Chapter of Rev. than any ten times as many verses in the whole Bible, & would not exchange the noble enthusiasm with which they inspire me, for all that this world has to offer.[2]

Burns's letters are always strongly influenced by the desire to engage, please or persuade the addressee yet, nonetheless, this has a ring of melancholic sincerity.

[1] W. E. Henley (ed.), *The Complete Writings of Robert Burns* (London: The Waverley Book Co., 1927), Vol. II, pp. 127–8.
[2] Ibid., Vol. VII, p. 34.

At the same moment, Robert was coming to terms with a rejection in love, probably by Alison Begbie, and this concatenation of depressions produced 'To Ruin'.

And thou grim pow'r, by life abhorr'd,
While life a pleasure can afford,
      O hear a wretch's pray'r
No more I shrink, appall'd, afraid;
I court, I beg thy friendly aid,
      To close this scene of care!
When shall my soul, in silent peace,
      Resign life's joyless day?
My weary heart its throbbings cease,
      Cold-mould'ring in the clay?
            No fear more, no tear more
                  To stain my lifeless face,
            Enclasped and grasped
                  Within thy cold embrace![3]

The same note is sounded in 'A Prayer, in the Prospect of Death' and 'Winter, a Dirge' which Burns described as the earliest of his poems to be printed.

Thou power supreme, whose mighty scheme
These woes of mine fulfil,
Here, firm I rest, they must be best,
Because they are Thy will!
Then all I want (O do Thou grant
This one request of mine!)

[3] Ibid., Vol. I, p. 291.

Since to enjoy Thou dost deny,
Assist me to resign.[4]

It is perhaps hard to take these youthful lugubrations entirely seriously and Burns himself was later to disown this self-confessedly bathetic emotional stage. Nonetheless, the point is that his natural language for expressing such emotions was religious.

The quotation from Alexander Pope in the letter to William Burnes is, however, also significant. The reference points were widening beyond the Biblical or theological, and Pope's version of Enlightenment Christianity became important to Burns because it was a poet's vision. Scholars such as Kenneth Simpson have analysed the references in Robert's letters to his early reading. These include, on the religious front, John Taylor's *The Scripture Doctrine of Original Sin* and James Hervey's Puritan and melancholic *Meditations*, in addition to Stackhouse's *Bible History*. We can also safely presume John Bunyan's *The Pilgrim's Progress* and Thomas Boston's *Fourfold State* as having an assured place in William Burnes's small but precious book collection. But on a wider literary front, Addison, Pope, Shakespeare, John Locke's *An Essay Concerning Human Understanding*, James Thomson, William Shenstone, Allan Ramsay, Robert Fergusson, Laurence Sterne and Henry Mackenzie all rate specific mentions.

The expansion of Robert's reading and ideas follows the Burnes family's move in 1777 from Mount Oliphant

[4] Ibid., Vol. I, p. 283.

to Lochlie, a 130-acre farm on the north bank of the River Ayr, near Tarbolton. The opportunities here for socialising were much greater than at the isolated Mount Oliphant and, in 1780, Burns was instrumental in the setting up of the Tarbolton Bachelor's Club which was designed to provide diversion from the 'necessary labours of life'.

In 1781, Robert saw more of these labours in his ultimately fruitless spell as a flex dresser in Irvine but, following his return to Lochlie in 1782, Robert renewed his social contacts and also increased his involvement with the St James (Tarbolton) Masonic Lodge. These fellowships bridged and, to some degree, cushioned a family crisis in 1783 when William was evicted and Mossgiel, near Mauchline, became the third and last farm to be taken on by Burns's now worn-down and ailing father. In the same year, the aspirant poet self-consciously began his first Commonplace Book which was a favoured Enlightenment method of reflecting on one's reading and cultivating self-improvement.

Out of the melancholy disappointments of 1781–2, the young Burns forged a new beginning which stimulated his early love songs and the first poems animated by a distinctive authorial persona. This change of attitude can be pinpointed in the 1782 song 'My Father was a Farmer':

My father was a farmer upon the Carrick border O,
And carefully he bred me, in decency and order O.
He bade me act a manly part, though I had ne'er a farthing O,
For without an honest manly heart, no man was worth
    regarding O.

Then out into the world my course I did determine, O,
Tho' to be rich was not my wish, yet to be great was
    charming O.
My talents they were not the worst, nor yet my education, O –
Resolv'd was I, at least to try, to mend my situation, O.

In many a way, and vain essay, I courted Fortune's favour, O
Some cause unseen, still stept between, to frustrate each
    endeavour, O
Sometimes by foes I was o'erpower'd, sometimes by friends
    forsaken, O
And when my hope was at the top, I still was worst
    mistaken, O.

Then sore harass'd, and tir'd at last, with Fortune's vain
    delusion, O,
I dropt my schemes, like idle dreams; and came to this
    conclusion, O –
The past was bad, and the future hid; its good or ill untried, O
But the present hour was in my pow'r, and so I would enjoy
    it, O.[5]

Inevitably, this moment of reorientation and renewal is measured against the paternal inheritance. Robert claims the mantle of his father's values, but the sociability to which he was now committing himself was foreign to William Burnes's determined and often lonely dedication.

The young poet's expanding frames of reference are charted in his verse epistles, eight of which featured in the *Kilmarnock Edition*, nine if one includes the 'Dedication

[5] Ibid., Vol. V, pp. 228–9.

to Gavin Hamilton'. The verse epistle is a classical poetic convention which was revived in English and Scottish eighteenth-century poetry to celebrate friendship and express a community of values. Through Robert's contributions to this genre we can see whom he counted as his peers in Ayrshire, and the kind of relationships he was forming. Throughout his life, Burns developed his ideas through his relationships and there is a close connection between his poetry and his devotion to letter writing. He is a master of the art in prose as well as poetry.

John Rankine was a farmer near Tarbolton, a wit and a convivial fellow drinker. He was also, according to Robert, a satiric critic of the Puritan clergy.

Ye hae sae monie cracks an' cants,	stories and jokes
And in your wicked drucken rants,	drunken
Ye mak a devil of the saints,	
An' fill them fou';	drunk
And then their failings, flaws, an' wants	
Are a' seen thro'.	

Hypocrisy, in mercy spare it!	
That holy robe, O dinna tear it!	
Spare 't for their sakes, wha aften wear it –	
The lads in black,	
But your curst wit, when it comes near it,	
Rives 't aff their back.[6]	tears

The main point, though, of Burns's 'Epistle to John Rankine' is a comic conceit linking hunting and poaching to his

[6] Ibid., Vol. II, p. 41.

liaison with Betty Paton which resulted in her pregnancy. The clergy need to be mocked since Burns has already run foul of the Kirk Session at Mauchline Church, presided over by the formidable 'Daddy Auld', a champion of conservative moral and theological values. Nothing could signal more clearly Robert's confrontational assertion of a freedom he had repressed during his father's final illness earlier in 1784.

The 'Epistle to Davie, a Brother Poet' runs on more literary tracks as befits David Sillar, a fellow bard of Ayrshire. The moral theme of the poem is the contrast between virtuous lack and immoral excess. The consolation of the poor, not least for poets, is the free appreciation of nature's bounty and the truths taught by misfortune. Moreover, friendship and love are the motivating powers of the universe, which unite the two poets with their lovers and with each other.

O all ye pow'rs who rule above!
O Thou, whose very self is love.[7]

Burns wrote a series of verse epistles to another older Ayrshire poet, John Lapraik, whose life was marred by a succession of money troubles. Again, the intention is to outline common literary and humane values.

Gie me ae spark o' nature's fire
That's a' the learning I desire;
Then, tho' I drudge thro' dub an' mire   puddle
*   At pleugh or cart,*   plough

[7] Ibid., Vol. I, p. 265.

My muse, tho' hamely in attire,
        May touch the heart.[8]

The second epistle laments the restrictions placed on poetry by unremitting physical labour but goes on to defy worldly wealth and pride in the name of 'wit an' sense' and human fellowship. These, avers Burns, are the writ of Heaven and what nature intended.

For thus the royal mandate ran,
When first the human race began:
'the social, friendly, honest man,
        Whate'er he be,
'Tis he fulfils great nature's plan,
        And none but he.'[9]

Social, friendly, honest women form, at this point in Robert's life, a slightly different category but his ideas on that were to evolve. What is most important is the affirmation that social and personal relations based on honesty provide the best measure of moral truth and wellbeing.

That core perception binds together two ideas that are revisited in 'To William Simson, Ochiltree'. First of all, moral truths realised in community require a local poetry, not abstract universality.

Th' Illissus, Tiber, Thames, an' Seine,
Glide sweet in monie a tunefu' line:

[8] Ibid., Vol. II, pp. 18–19.
[9] Ibid., Vol. II, pp. 27–8.

But, Willie, set your fit to mine,
*   An' cock your crest!*
We'll gar our streams and burnies shine   make
*   Up wi' the best.*[10]

Secondly, humane, social truth of this kind exposes the dogmatic theological assertions as, at best, lacking in truthfulness and, at worst, as a mask for hypocrisy.

The impression given by the authorial persona in Burns's Verse Epistles is of a young man who has grown up fast, able to give as well as receive moral insights. These range from the supreme importance of pleasure in the 'Epistle to James Smith' to the supreme value of true religion in the 'Epistle to a Young Friend'. Are these contradictory perspectives?

James Smith was a very close friend of Burns's young adulthood in Mauchline and an intimate of his artistic and sexual tribulations. Pleasure is their 'magic wand' against age and time, but also the catalyst of emotion and the pulse of life.

O ye douce folk that live by rule,   respectable
Grave, tideless-blooded, calm an' cool,
Compar'd wi' you – O fool! fool! fool!
*   How much unlike!*
Your hearts are just a standing pool,
*   Your lives, a dyke!*[11]   stone wall

[10] Ibid., Vol. II, p. 32.
[11] Ibid., Vol. I, p. 199.

The 'Young Friend' receives a more prudential perspective in the light of egotism, the cash nexus and illicit sex. True independence demands respect for self and others and the practice of true religion.

The great Creator to revere
　　　　Must sure become the Creature;
But still the preaching cant forbear,
　　　　And ev'n the rigid feature:
Yet ne'er with wits profane to rage
　　　　Be complaisance extended;
An atheist-laugh's a poor exchange
　　　　For Deity offended!

When ranting round in pleasure's ring,
　　　　Religion may be blinded;
Or if she gie a random fling,
　　　　It may be little minded;
But when on Life we're tempest-driv'n
　　　　A Conscience but a canker –
A correspondence fix'd wi' Heav'n
　　　　Is sure a noble anchor![12]

The difference between these two Epistles is one of emphasis and of selection. In each case, Burns is guided by whom he is writing to and the need to communicate appropriately. He has the grace to acknowledge to his young correspondent that he has not always lived up to his own advice. The Verse Epistles do not provide a moral system but moral

[12] Ibid., Vol. I, pp. 295–6, amended.

conversations, a process that contextualises and articulates the truths of experience through relationships.

In these regards the Verse Epistles offer a grounding for the rest of Burns's early poetry, which is embodied in the *Kilmarnock Edition* of 1786 and in the significant exclusions from that volume. But this background is often obscured by the brilliance of the foreground fireworks. Burns's social satires combine a robust inventiveness with an ebullient brio of execution, all laced with humour. 'The Twa Dogs' which opens the *Kilmarnock* collection sets a tone with the superbly comic dialogue between the lower-class and upper-class canine cronies. The satire, though, is double-edged since, unlike their masters, the 'twa dugs' relate well and sympathise with each other in a way that proves humans can and should conduct themselves better, rather than that dogs may be better 'best friends' than people.

The same interchange of beast and human underlies 'The Death and Dying Words of Poor Mailie', the poet's pet ewe. As Mailie expires she instructs her master in improved animal husbandry and commends her offspring to his tender, watchful care. This is parody but not wholly, since what the animal commends is how humans should behave to each other.

And now, my bairns, wi' my last breath,	
I lea'e my blessin wi' you baith:	both
An' when you think upo' your mither,	mother
Mind to be kind to ane anither.[13]	another

---

[13] Ibid., Vol. I, p. 187.

Both poems, of course, also embody local situations and local language, so exemplifying the models advocated in the Verse Epistles. 'To A Louse' is a further sally in the same style of pungent social comment. The louse which the poet addresses is crawling up Miss Jenny's Sunday bonneted head with no sense of either Sabbath decorum or the lady's evident self-regard. Again, of course, the wit is double-edged since the insect's disregard for rank or social airs shows up human vanity and short-sightedness. How on earth can a louse be so oblivious of the distinction between an old wife's bonnet and this fashionable hairdo topped with the best Sunday headgear? The moral drawn by the poet, in lieu of listening to the sermon, is often quoted without Burns's compelling context.

O wad some power the giftie gie us
To see oursels as ithers see us!
It wad frae monie a blunder free us;   from many
        An' foolish notion:
What airs in dress an' gait wad lea'e us,   leave
        An' ev'n devotion![14]

'Death and Doctor Hornbook' is another comic dialogue narrating, this time, an encounter between the poet and Death himself. Death's complaint is that the local Tarbolton schoolteacher (hence the reference to the hornbook of elementary education) has taken to selling medicines as a sideline. He is moreover foolishly proud of his medicinal skills. The result is not, as one might hope, an increase in

[24] Ibid., Vol. II, p. 13.

those evading death through medical treatment, but an increase in those expiring without Death's intervention, so depriving him of his 'lawfu' prey'. This poem circulated freely in Ayrshire but had to await the *Edinburgh Edition* of 1787 for formal publication. Its real-life subject, John Wilson, was still the schoolmaster at Tarbolton, a member of the Kirk Session and a fellow Mason. The satire is direct and deadly.

Exactly the same could be said of a series of religious satires conceived by Burns during this first astonishing outburst of creative maturity, though some were only published later and some posthumously. The first of these 'parish poems' is 'The Twa Herds' or 'The Holy Tulzie' in which Burns lampoons a furious fall-out between two ministers concerning their respective parish boundaries. It is a typically Presbyterian dispute but the piquancy of this unseemly brawl can only be savoured by those who know that both parties, Rev. Alexander Moodie and Rev. John Russell, are conservative Calvinists who should be uniting to repel the modernisers.

O a' ye pious, godly flocks
Weel fed on pastures orthodox,
Wha now will keep you frae the fox
   Or worryin tykes?   dogs
Or wha will tent the waifs an' crocks stragglers / old ewes
   About the dykes!

The twa best herds in a' the wast,   west
That e'er gae gospel horn a blast
These five an' twenty simmers past,
   O dool to tell!   sorrow

Hae had a bitter, black out cast	falling out
Atween themsel.[15]	between

Burns's satire is doubly effective since he writes ironically from the perspective of the 'Auld Licht' purists, who would now be defenceless were it not for the staunch fulminations of Burns's own (and least favourite) minister at Mauchline, Rev. William Auld.

This is partisan pleading which requires local knowledge to be appreciated. The background to the poet's campaigning posture is provided in his 'Epistle to John Goldie', which celebrates a notable lay theologian of Kilmarnock whose 'The Gospel Recovered' is, claims Burns, 'terror o the Whigs / Dread o black coats and reverend wigs'. Goldie's fault, according to the conservative Calvinists, is his application of reason to Protestant beliefs. In this he was following in the footsteps of John Taylor's *The Scripture Doctrine of Original Sin* which also featured in Burns's early theological reading and to which he refers in the 'Epistle'.

'Tis you an' Taylor are the chief
To blame for a this black mischief.[16]

The 'mischief' involves putting Biblical texts in their wider context, distinguishing clearly between literal and meta-phorical or figurative meanings, and applying human self-understanding at all points.

[15] Ibid., Vol. II, p. 275.
[16] Ibid., Vol. III, p. 55.

Goldie, however, goes further in setting God's goodness and perfection as a standard against which Christian doctrines should be measured. In consequence, key Calvinist teachings, such as the total corruption of human nature due to original sin, and predestination to heaven or hell, are vigorously discarded as not in keeping with the Bible as 'the Word of God'. The tactic here is to out-Protestantise the Calvinists by appealing to the supreme source of religious authority in the Reformation tradition, Holy Scripture, 'correctly interpreted'.

This theological underpinning is transmitted in 'Holy Willie's Prayer' into a brilliant dramatic monologue. Again, there is a specific local occasion: the attempt by Mauchline Kirk's Puritan conservatives, enthusiastically supported by Rev. Auld, to arraign one of the community's leading citizens, Gavin Hamilton (Burns's landlord, friend and patron), on charges of moral laxness and the mishandling of charitable funds. The partisan and personalised nature of this assault is evident, but Hamilton was no pushover and taking his case, with professional legal assistance, to both Presbytery and Synod he soundly trounced the Mauchline Session who were compelled to delete the critical judgements from their minutes. Nothing is so humiliating in Presbyterianism as being forced to strike out an official decision by a higher ecclestiastical court.

Burns captures this moment through the supposed consciousness of William Fisher, chief among the Puritan faction. It is no surprise that this widely circulated monologue remained unpublished during the poet's lifetime since, even today, it would be wide open to a libel suit. Not only is Fisher condemned from his own mouth as an oily humbug, but he is explicitly accused of sexual misconduct and hypocrisy. Worst of all, Burns's searing satiric art slides seamlessly from theology to lust with the movement of Fisher's thoughts.

> *But yet – O Lord – confess I must –*
> *At times I'm fash'd wi' fleshly lust;*   troubled
> *And sometimes too, in wardly trust,*
>   *Vile self gets in;*
> *But Thou remembers we are dust,*
>   *Defiled wi' sin.*

> *Oh Lord, yestreen – Thou kens – wi' Meg –*
> *Thy pardon I sincerely beg –*
> *O may't ne'er be a living plague,*
> *To my dishonour!*
> *An' I'll ne'er lift a lawless leg*
> *Again upon her.*[17]

The achievement of 'Holy Willie's Prayer' is to create a convincing comic monster whose rhetoric transcends the poem's origins and indeed its partisan points. Nonetheless, the theology of Taylor and Goldie is specifically undermining the Calvinist claim to 'election' by God regardless of moral merit. Fisher is 'a chosen sample' and even his sexual peccadilloes can be viewed by him as confirmation of this elect status.

> *Maybe Thou lets this fleshly thorn*
> *Buffet Thy servant e'en and morn,*

[17] Ibid., Vol. II, p. 284.

Lest he owre proud and high should turn,
That he's sae gifted;
If sae, Thy han' maun e'en be borne
Until Thou lift it.[18]

This claim to divine partiality spills over into the Old Testament-style expectation that God should crush the enemies of the 'chosen', in particular Gavin Hamilton and his lawyer Robert Aitken. Again, Burns's monologue elides any distinction between 'high' religious principle and petty vindictiveness. The effect is devastating and, though now primarily valued for its humour, 'Holy Willie's Prayer' must have enraged as much as it amused. Burns dismisses Fisher in the Glenriddell manuscript as an 'Elder in the parish of Mauchline and much, and justly, famed for that polemical chattering which ends in tippling Orthodoxy and for that Spiritualised Bawdry which refines to Liquorish Devotion'. Perhaps the Mauchline elder was able to console himself as one of those blessed by unrighteous persecution. The poor man died years later having fallen into a ditch, drunk.

Burns's assault on the religiously rigid is justified in 'A Dedication to Gavin Hamilton' and again in 'To the Rev. John M'Math' who succeeded the Rev. Patrick Woodrow as the minister of Tarbolton. Both men were modernisers and Burns expects a sympathetic hearing for 'Holy Willie's Prayer' while acknowledging that he may have overstepped the conventional mark.

[18] Ibid., Vol. II, pp. 284–5.

I own 'twas rash, an' rather hardy,
That I, a simple, countra Bardie,
Should meddle wi' a pack sae sturdy,
            Wha, if they ken me;
Can easy, wi' a single wordie,
            Louse Hell upon me.   loose

But I gae mad at their grimaces
Their sighan, cantan, grace-prood faces,
Their three-mile prayers, an' hauf-mile graces,
            Their raxin conscience,   stretching
Whase greed, revenge, an' pride disgraces
            Waur nor their nonsense.[19]   worse

Burns's argument is that he has not assaulted true faith but those who 'take Religion in their mouth' only to deny mercy, grace and truth in their actions.

All hail Religion! Maid divine!
Pardon a muse sae mean as mine,
Who in her rough imperfect line
            Thus daurs to name thee;   dares
To stigmatise false friends of thine
            Can ne'er defame thee.[20]

It is important to remember that this 'Epistle' is directed to a clergyman and that Burns's epistolary art aims to please. Nonetheless, the argument links back to Goldie's theology, and his characterisation of the righteous as failing in true

[19] Ibid., Vol. III, pp. 61–2.
[20] Ibid., Vol. III, p. 64.

Protestantism. In the poem's words, the Puritan faction apply 'Their jugglin, hocus-pocus arts / To cheat the crowd' like, by implication, Roman Catholic priests, which was not a favoured comparison in Calvinist circles. By contrast, Burns hails the McMaths and Woodrows:

O Ayr! my dear, my native ground,
Within thy presbyterial bound
A candid lib'ral band is found
           Of public teachers,
As men, as Christians too renown'd
           An manly preachers.[21]

The partisan vein is continued in poems such as 'The Kirk's Alarm' without the dramatic brio of 'Holy Willie's Prayer'. But Burns was to produce two further satires on religious life in Ayrshire which are more ambivalent in tone and effect. 'The Ordination' homes in on the vexed issue of 'patronage', or the appointment of ministers by landed proprietors regardless of the congregation's wishes. The catalyst is the 'intrusion' by the landed patron, the Earl of Glencairn, of a modernising minister Rev. James Mackinlay into Kilmarnock's Laigh Kirk. This is violently opposed by popular protest which leads, in turn, to repression by the civic authorities including the whipping of protestors through the streets as an example.

Burns writes with the perspective and energy of the populist revolt and, though he is satirising the conservative

---

[21] Ibid., Vol. III, p. 65.

attack on the 'New Light', his vigorous rhythms also give outlet to the energies of this anarchic uprising, as does his raw colloquial language.

> *Mak haste an' turn King David owre,*   look up Psalm
>   *An' lilt wi' holy clangor;*
> *O' double verse come gie us four,*
>   *An' skirl up the* Bangor: pipe up tune
> *This day the Kirk kicks up a stoure,*   dust
>   *Nae mair the knaves shall wrang her,*
> *For Heresy is in her pow'r,*
>   *And gloriously she'll whang her*   strike
>   *Wi pith this day.*[22]

A paradox begins to emerge in 'The Ordination' since, although Burns's religious sympathies lie with the patron's choice of minister, his growing political instincts tend towards the protestors. To put this dispute in context, the electorate of Ayrshire at that time numbered 224 male property owners, about 100 of whom were substantial lairds. In practice the eight earls, who as peers had no vote, arranged the election of the county MP and of a further MP for the Ayrshire burghs. By contrast, popular defiance of the parallel process by which ministers were appointed is remarkable, yet perhaps not so remarkable when the strong Covenanting association between conservative Puritanism and political radicalism is remembered. In point of fact, some key thinkers on the modernising wing of Scottish Protestantism such as Francis Hutcheson had also been opposed to patronage.

[22] Ibid., Vol. II, p. 32.

Politics and religion intertwined in other arenas of the Ayrshire community. Freemasonry in the eighteenth century was one of the few contexts in which men of different social classes met on an equal footing; even in Church, attenders were segregated by pews allocated according to social and economic status. Ideals of brotherhood and equality were central to Freemasonry and had considerable political influence, not least on Burns. However, Freemasonry is also a form of religion with codified beliefs, initiation rituals and ceremonies.

In the nature of Freemasonry, emphasis is placed on what is shared in private fellowship rather than what is publicly broadcast. This secrecy protected the sharing of radical opinions. Nonetheless, Burns did publish an (anticipated) 'Farewell to the Brethren of St James's Lodge, Tarbolton', written at that critical juncture in his life before publication of the *Kilmarnock Edition*. The 'Farewell' is a classic celebration of good fellowship.

Oft have I met your social Band,
    And spent the cheerful, festive night;
Oft, honour'd with supreme command,
    Presided o'er the Sons of Light;
And by that Hieroglyphic *bright,*
    Which none but Craftsmen *ever saw!*
Strong Mem'ry on my heart shall write
    Those happy scenes when far awa.[23]

---

[23] Ibid., Vol. II, pp. 54–5, amended.

Burns picks up on these specific references to Masonic symbolism from ancient Egypt and Israel and proceeds to articulate the core belief of Freemasonry in an immortal, omniscient, ordering, benevolent God who desires freedom, harmony and love for humankind.

May Freedom, Harmony and Love,
    Unite you in the Grand Design,
Beneath th' Omniscient Eye above,
    The glorious Architect *Divine!*
That you may keep th' Unerring Line,
    Still rising by the Plummet's Law,
Till Order *bright completely shine,*
    Shall be my pray'r when far awa.[24]

This guiding belief resurfaces again and again in Burns's poems and letters throughout his life.

It is significant that Robert's involvement in the Tarbolton Lodge, which dates from 1781, coincides with the decisive and formative period of his early twenties. In these years he stepped out from his father's shadow, overcame a significant setback in Irvine, and developed a poetic voice of astonishing maturity and poise. In 1784, Burns became Depute Master of the St James Lodge and his close association with Freemasonry continued through the Edinburgh visits, where the social networks of the Lodge were critical to promoting Robert as a 'national bard'. Freemasonry provided a vital social and intellectual environment in which the poet's values and beliefs evolved.

[24] Ibid., Vol. II, p. 55.

As Burns's more settled Ayrshire years came to a close, he was producing poetry of dramatic and linguistic excellence, delivered with metrical and technical sophistication. These qualities are on full display in the local poetry as a whole and in the Kirk satires, but they culminate in two outstanding works of festivity and fellowship, 'The Holy Fair' and 'Love and Liberty'.

'The Holy Fair' describes a communion season or 'occasion' in Mauchline when people gathered from neighbouring areas to hear a succession of preachers and, if permitted by conscience and social reputation, to receive communion. Due to the numbers involved – up to two or even three thousand people might congregate – these events were held outdoors. Thomas Crawford quotes extensively from an eye-witness account of a Communion Season written by a blacksmith. Robert Chambers suggested this as a possible source for the poem though, of course, Burns himself was closely acquainted with such events.

> In Scotland they run from kirk to kirk, and flock to see a sacrament, and make the same use of it that the papists do of their pilgrimages and processions; that is, indulge themselves in drunkenness, folly, and idleness … At the time of the administration of the Lord's Supper upon the Thursday, Saturday and Monday, we have preaching in the fields near the church. At first, you find a great number of men and women lying together upon the grass; here they are sleeping and snoring, some with their faces towards heaven, others with their faces turned downwards, or covered with their bonnets; there you find a knot of young fellows and girls making assignations to go home together in the evening, or

to meet in some ale-house; in another place you see a pious circle sitting round an ale-barrel, many of which stand ready upon carts for the refreshment of the saints ... in this sacred assembly there is an odd mixture of religion, sleep, drinking, courtship, and a confusion of sexes, ages and characters. When you get a little nearer the speaker, so as to be within the reach of the sound, though not of the sense of the words, for that can only reach a small circle, you will find some weeping and others laughing, some pressing to get nearer the tent or tub in which the parson is sweating, bawling, jumping and beating the desk; others fainting with the stifling heat, or wrestling to extricate themselves from the crowd; one seems very devout and serious, and the next moment is scolding and cursing his neighbour for squeezing or treading on him; in an instant after, his countenance is composed to the religious gloom, and he is groaning, sighing, and weeping for his sins: in a word, there is such an absurd mixture of the serious and comic that, were we convened for any other purpose than that of worshipping the God and Governor of Nature, the scene would exceed all *power of face*.[25]

In literary terms, 'The Holy Fair' continues a great succession of folk festivity poems in Scots, reaching back to the medieval era and recently renewed by eighteenth-century works such as Robert Fergusson's 'Leith Races'. There are similarities also with Burns's 'Hallowe'en'. However, the poem begins with a narrative impetus setting the scene and describing the narrator's encounter one fine Sunday morning 'early on the road'.

[25] Robert Chambers (ed.), *The Life and Works of Robert Burns*, as revised by William Wallace (Edinburgh and London: W. & R. Chambers, 1896), Vol. I, pp. 268–9.

Upon a simmer Sunday morn,
    When Nature's face is fair,
I walked forth to view the corn,
    An' snuff the caller air: fresh
The rising sun, owre Galston Muirs,
    Wi' glorious light was glintin;
The hares were hirplin down the furs, going crookedly / furrows
    The lav'rocks they were chantin   larks
        Fu' sweet that day.   full

As lightsomely I glowr'ed abroad,
    To see a scene sae gay,
Three hizzies, early at the road,   wenches
    Cam skelpan up the way.   hurrying
Twa had manteeles o' dolefu' black,   two / mantles
    But any wi' lyart lining;   grey
The third, that gaed a wee aback,
    Was in the fashion shining
        Fu' gay that day.[26]

Things move in an allegorical direction when the three ladies
are introduced as 'Fun', 'Superstition' and 'Hypocrisy'.

This prelude then yields to a description of the anything but solemn gathering, since the godly are rather
outnumbered by the idle, the curious and those in search
of carnal, rather than heavenly, experiences. Nonetheless,
the main business proceeds with a series of preachers,
each striving to excel before these unusually massed ranks.
The Calvinist traditionalists such as Russell and Moodie

[26] Henley, Vol. I, pp. 161–6.

(familiar from other Kirk satires) call down damnation on the sinners.

Hear how he clears the points o' Faith
      Wi' rattlin and thumpin!
Now meekly calm, now wild in wrath,
      He's stampin, an' he's jumpin!
His lengthen'd chin, his turn'd-up snout,
      His eldritch squeel an' gestures   unearthly
O how they fire the heart devout,
      Like cantharidian plaisters
            On sic a day![27]

Cantharidian plasters produced blisters, and Moodie's comic antics may themselves have done the preacher a physical injury.

Then, however, Rev. George Smith enters the preachers' shelter, or tent, to lecture on morality and reason. This does not please the crowd as even the idlers expect a dose of real old-time religion and not modernising moral philosophy.

But hark! the tent has chang'd its voice;
      There's peace an' rest nae langer;   no longer
For a' the real judges rise,
      They canna sit fur anger:
Smith opens out his cauld harangues,
      On practice and on morals,
An' aff the godly pour in throngs,

[27] Ibid., Vol. I, p. 167.

> *To gie the jars an' barrels*
>   *A lift that day.*

What signifies his barren shine,
    Of moral pow'rs an' reason;
His English style, an' gesture fine
    Are a' clean out o' season.
Like Socrates or Antonine,
    Or some auld pagan heathen,
The moral man he does define,
    But ne'er a word o' faith in
        That's right that day.[28]

In the poem's terms, Old and New Lights are equally satirised, since the narrator adopts a general mood or perspective. This renders 'The Holy Fair' a more detached and less partisan work than 'Holy Willie's Prayer' or even 'The Ordination'.

    The narrative follows through the day's proceedings as theological discussion switches to the taverns and, finally, to social merriment and sexual encounter.

Some swagger hame the best they dow,	can
Some wait the afternoon.	
At slaps the billies halt a blink,	gaps in wall
Till lasses strip their shoon:	shoes
Wi' faith an' hope, an love an' drink,	
They're a' in famous tune	
For crack that day.[29]	gossip

[28] Ibid, Vol. I, pp. 167–8.
[29] Ibid, Vol. I, p. 173.

What kind of communion has taken place? Spiritual?
Bacchanalian? Erotic? For Burns, the three have merged.

How monie hearts this day converts	many
O' sinners and o' lasses!	
Their hearts o' stane, gin night, are gane	gone
As saft as onie flesh is:	
There's some are fou o' love divine;	full
There's some are fou o' brandy;	
An' monie jobs that day begin,	
May end in Houghmagandie	sexual intercourse
Some ither day.[30]	other

The humorist in Burns traces here the continuation of popular
folk religion despite Puritan denial and Enlightenment
reason. In this regard the Scottish poet also anticipates two
revolutionary cultural movements, Romanticism and the
related Evangelical impulse towards a religion of the heart.
The nineteenth century would see such occasions turn to
outpourings of revivalist emotion.

The conclusion of 'The Holy Fair' also points towards
the Bacchanalian festivity of 'Love and Liberty', in which
beggars, cairds or tinkers, former soldiers and landless
wanderers gather at Poosie Nansie's low-class tavern in
Mauchline for a night of carefree drinking, sexual licence
and superb entertainment in music and song. This is a
concelebration of outsiders, a religion of passion and excess
which denies all social restraints in a visceral hymn to
freedom. At the same time, the dramatic construction of the

[30] Ibid., Vol. I, pp. 173–4.

piece is intense and the complex metrical variations display dazzling technical virtuosity. It took Matthew Arnold, an outsider to Scottish poetry and social respectability, to salute the true stature of a work which, tragically, remained unpublished in Burns's lifetime.

> In the world of *The Jolly Beggars* there is more than hideousness and squalor, there is bestiality; yet the piece is a superb poetic success. It has breadth, truth and power which make its famous scene in Auerbach's cellar, of Goethe's *Faust*, seem artificial and tame beside it, and which are matched only by Shakespeare and Aristophanes.[31]

In 'Love and Liberty' there is no place for the structures of institutional religion in any of its guises. The poet harnesses and disciplines the ecstatic power of the Bacchanal by and for art alone, while revelling in the company of the sinners and outcasts. All else is exposed as a form of hypocrisy.

See the smoking bowl before us,
Mark our jovial, ragged ring!
Round and round take up the chorus,
And in raptures let us sing –

A fig for those by law protected!
Liberty's a glorious feast
Courts for Cowards were erected,
Churches built to please the priest.[32]

---

[31] Quoted in Andrew Scott and Patrick Scott Hogg (eds), *The Canongate Burns* (Edinburgh: Canongate Classics, 2001), p. 589.
[32] Henley, Vol. II, pp. 271–2.

As Robert left Mauchline, not for the West Indies as originally intended but for Edinburgh, he was a fully-formed radical artist heading for a very conservative capital city.

Chapter Four

Justice and Compassion

Gilbert Burns was limited and discreet in what he contributed to the first official and rather problematic biography of his brother Robert by James Currie, but he did vividly convey the economic and emotional pressures under which the boys grew up.

> We lived very sparingly. For several years butcher's meat was a stranger in the house, while all the members of the family exerted themselves to the utmost of their strength, and rather beyond it in the labours of the farm. My brother at the age of thirteen assisted in threshing the crop of corn, and at fifteen was the principal labourer on the farm, for we had no hired servant, male or female. The anguish of mind we felt at our tender years, our father growing old (for he was now above fifty) broken down with the long continued fatigues of his life, with a wife and five other children, and in a declining state of circumstances, these reflections produced in my brother's mind and mine sensations of the deepest distress. I doubt not but the hard labour and sorrow of this period of his life, was in a great measure the cause of that depression of spirits with which Robert was so often afflicted through his whole life afterwards.[1]

[1] James Currie (ed.), *The Works of Robert Burns* (Liverpool, 1800), Vol. I, p. 61.

The Burns family were well treated by some landlords but also experienced the impersonal harassment of factors (the landowners' agent) intent on enforcing contracts to the letter. In later life, Robert recalled with distress and fury the whole family being reduced to tears by the receipt of bullying letters demanding payment on the threat of eviction.

Life on a small farm, however straitened, was infinitely preferable to destitution, with its choice between the poor-house or the existence of itinerant homeless beggars. Poverty of this kind inevitably meant the break-up of a family which was the very thing William Burnes had struggled to avoid. This point is at the heart of an early song of Robert's called 'The Ruined Farmer' which was published only after his death:

There lies the dear partner of my breast;
Her cares for a moment at rest:
Must I see thee, my youthful pride,
        Thus brought so very low!
And it's O, fickle Fortune, O!

There lie my sweet babies in her arms
No anxious fear their little hearts alarms;
But for their sake my heart does ache,
        With many a bitter throe:
And it's O, fickle fortune, O![2]

The intertwining themes of poverty, oppression and justice are taken up by Burns from the beginning of his poetic

---

[2] W. E. Henley (ed.), *The Complete Writings of Robert Burns* (London: The Waverley Book Co., 1927), Vol. V, pp. 217–18.

development, and they are integral to his fashioning a truthful response to the sum of experience and environment. They thread through the Verse Epistles and are clearly articulated in the local satires such as 'The Twa Dogs'. At the very start of the *Kilmarnock Edition* Burns states his radical critique, albeit in disarmingly humorous mode.

LUATH

Trowth, Caesar, whyles they're fash'd eneugh:	truly / harassed
A cotter howkin in a sheugh,	digging / ditch
Wi' dirty stanes biggin a dyke,	stones / building
Bairin a quarry, an' sic like,	opening
Himsel, a wife, he thus sustains,	
A smytrie o' wee duddie weans,	litter / ragged children
An' nought but his han'-darg to keep	hand's labour
Them right an' tight in thack an' raep.	thatch and binding
An' when they meet wi' sair disasters,	sore
Like loss o' health or want o' masters,	
Ye maist wad think, a wee touch langer,	most / would
An' they maun starve o' cauld and hunger:	must / cold
But how it comes, I never kend yet,	learned
They're mostly wonderfu' contented;	
An' buirdly chiels, an' clever hizzies,	well-built men / women
Are bred in sic a way as this is.[3]	such

The cunning of the satiric method here is that Luath, the ploughman's collie, muzzles his critique by pointing to the contentment of the honest peasant. It is left to Caesar,

[3] Ibid., Vol. I, p. 133, amended.

the high-class hound, to describe direct oppression and harassment.

CAESAR
But then tae see how ye're negleckit,
How huff'd, an' cuff'd, an' disrespeckit!
Lord man, our gentry care as little
For delvers, ditchers, an' sic cattle;
They gang as saucy by poor folk,
As I wad by a stinkin brock.   badger

I've noticed on our Laird's court-day,
(An' monie a time's my heart's been wae),   many / woe
Poor tenant bodies, scant o' cash,
How they mon thole a factor's snash: bear / abuse
He'll stamp an' threaten, curse an' swear
He'll apprehend them, poind their gear;
While they maun staun', wi' aspect humble,
An' fear it a', an' fear an' tremble!

I see how folk live that hae riches;
But surely poor-folk maun be wretches![4]   must

Burns's more earnest treatments of these themes do not always come off artistically ('A Winter's Night' being one example) but 'Man Was Made to Mourn' is a worthy representative in the *Kilmarnock Edition* of the poet's more sober and dignified strain. It is also a further demonstration of the young poet's literary sophistication and his later artistic influence. The poem begins with a setting that garners up

[4] Ibid., Vol. I, pp. 133–4.

eighteenth-century English elegy, localises it, and anticipates Wordsworth's *Lyrical Ballads*.

When chill November's surly blast
    Made fields and forests bare,
One ev'ning as I wand'red forth
    Along the banks of Ayr,
I spy'd a man, whose aged step
    Seem'd weary, worn with care,
His face was furrow'd o'er with years,
    And hoary was his hair.[5]

Wordsworth's Simon Lee and his leech gatherer follow in this tradition of oppressed souls who voice the wise yet sad truths of human experience. Again one senses the background presence of William Burnes, not least because the sage of the poem proceeds to challenge any fatalistic reading of 'Man Was Made to Mourn'. The conditions of life may be difficult but they are made much worse by wrongdoing, guilt and inhumanity.

Many and sharp the num'rous Ills
    Inwoven with our frame!
More pointed still we make ourselves
    Regret, remorse, and shame!
And Man, whose heav'n-erected face,
    The smiles of love adorn,
Man's inhumanity to Man
    Makes countless thousands mourn![6]

[5] Ibid., Vol. I, p. 277.
[6] Ibid., Vol. I, pp. 279–80.

Burns then develops this point through vivid – and familiar – illustration and by echoing a philosophy of equality and individual rights.

If I'm design'd yon lordling's slave –
  By nature's law design'd –
Why was an independent wish
  E'er planted in my mind?
If not, why am I subject to
  His cruelty, or scorn?
Or why has Man the will and pow'r
  To make his fellow mourn?[7]

Calvinist predeterminism is explicitly challenged in favour of the ability and right of human free will to exercise choice and effect change. The argument is not fully developed, but this is 'A Man's a Man for a' That' in the making. The poem ends on the assurance that there is also compassion and comfort in the world and that even death may come as a merciful release.

In Burns's mature poetry the demand for justice and the necessity for compassion are usually held together as two sides of the same moral view, but there are also angry bursts of invective like the improvised lines written by Robert on a bank-note in 1786, when he believed he would have to leave Scotland to seek a living overseas.

Wae worth thy power, thou cursed leaf!
Fell source of a' my woe and grief,

[7] Ibid., Vol. I, p. 280.

For lack o' thee I've lost my lass;
For lack o' thee I scrimp my glass;
I see the children of affliction
Unaided, through thy curs'd restriction;
I've seen th' oppressor's cruel smile
Amid his hapless victims' spoil;
And for thy potence vainly wish'd
To crush the villain in the dust:
For lack o' thee I leave this much-lov'd shore,
Never, perhaps to greet old Scotland more![8]

Any account of Burns's active political advocacy has to be qualified by the conditions of censorship under which he wrote, first in Ayrshire's managed society and later in the national climate of suppression engendered by the French Revolution of 1789. He was not at liberty to speak fully what he thought and felt. Nonetheless, it does not need a Sherlock Holmes to discern the clarity, consistency and passion of his radical stance.

Amid the early political poems are 'The Author's Earnest Cry and Prayer', an attack on excise duties imposed by the Westminster parliament, and the anti-Hanoverian 'The Dream'. Burns's early politics are not republican in any theoretical sense. Monarchy is a fact of political life and the poet praises the deposed Stewarts as a symbol of Scottish nationhood while attacking Hanoverianism's 'German Geordies' as representative of everything that is wrong with post-Union rule of Scotland from London. Written in 1786,

[8] Ibid., Vol. III, p. 253.

following George III's birthday, 'A Dream' is a risky piece which Burns was advised to exclude from the *Edinburgh Edition*, though he refused to comply.

For me! before a Monarch's face,
    Ev'n there I winna flatter;   will not
For neither Pension, Post, nor Place,
    Am I your humble debtor:
So, nae reflection on your Grace,
    Your Kingship to bespatter;
There's monie waur been o' the race,   many worse
    And aiblins ane been better   perhaps one
        Than you this day.[9]

This is bold enough but the poet goes on to scold the Prince of Wales for 'driving rarely / Down Pleasure's stream wi' swelling sails', while Prince William 'young, royal Tarry-breeks' is lampooned for his latest sexual excess as covered by the red-top newspapers of the time.

If 'A Dream' is on the borderline of printability, then 'A New Psalm' goes over the edge and was published anonymously in London's *Morning Star* in 1789. The occasion was an official day of thanksgiving for George III's recovery from insanity, and Burns's parodic Psalm is composed for the Calvinist Puritans to sing in church that day.

O sing a new song to the Lord!
    Make, all and every one,

[9] Ibid., Vol. I, p. 202.

A joyful noise, ev'n for the King
  His restoration –

…

Th' ungodly o'er the just prevail'd,
  For so thou hadst appointed,
That Thou mightst greater glory give,
  Unto Thine own anointed![10]

Of course, the point is double-barbed since the Calvinist Purists were averse to giving thanks for any King other than 'Jesus Christ, the King and Head of the Church'. Robert, in contrast, was by this time commissioned as an Excise Officer and obliged to maintain public loyalty. In fact, when Burns was lobbying in Edinburgh for the commission, the fiercely anti-Hanoverian lines scratched by him on the window near Stirling Castle in 1787 were cited against him. Though unpublished, they were well known.

Here Stewarts once in glory reign'd;
And laws for Scotland's weal ordain'd;
But now unroof'd their Palace stands,
Their sceptre's fallen to other hands;
Fallen indeed, and to the earth,
Whence grovelling reptiles take their birth!
The injured Stewart line are gone,
A race outlandish fill their throne;
An idiot race, to honour lost;
Who know them best despise them most.[11]

[10] Ibid., Vol. III, pp. 185–7.
[11] Ibid., Vol. IV, p. 14.

The poems already discussed undermine any idea that Burns's political radicalism developed later in response to the French Revolution. This point is well put by Thomas Crawford:

> Almost everything that Burns ever wrote was political, in the broadest sense of that word. Even his refurbishment of traditional love-songs can be subsumed under that head, for he regarded their collection and arrangement as a patriotic – that is, a political – act. The central core of all his thought was his exploration of the Scottish predicament; he belonged to a nation which had lost its independence but was at the same time part of a larger state in whose successes he could rejoice and in whose better government he was interested, so that his patriotism was always of a peculiarly double sort. His attachment to what, for want of a better word, must be termed his 'class' – that is, to the 'lower orders', broadly conceived – reinforced and buttressed his nationalism.[12]

The first paradigms of liberty for Robert Burns were William Wallace, Bruce and the historical struggle for Scottish freedom. But the poet's political ideas develop around four revolutions: the sixteenth-century Protestant Reformation, the 'Glorious Revolution' of 1688, the American War of Independence which coincided with his teenage years and, finally, the French Revolution with its accompanying upsurge in British radicalism and subsequent repressive reaction. Religion and political principles support each other throughout.

[12] Thomas Crawford, *Burns: A Study of the Poems and Songs* (Edinburgh: James Thin, 1978), p. 238.

For William Burnes and his sons, the Protestant Reformation was based on individual freedom of conscience which they regarded as the bedrock of liberty. No authority – royal, civil or ecclesiastical – had the right to overrule the just decrees of conscience, informed by divine guidance through the Bible. Any attempt to impose unjust, unrighteous or tyrannical commands was to be met by the right of resistance and, if necessary, by the overthrow of the unjust powers.

The theory of righteous resistance was propounded by Calvin but emphasised by John Knox and fully systematised by the Scottish scholar and poet George Buchanan. Revered throughout Europe, Buchanan was a leading and radical Christian Humanist who taught Montaigne and Ignatius Loyola. He was a Court Poet to Mary Queen of Scots in France and Scotland, but subsequently denounced her and notoriously sought her deposition and execution. As tutor to James VI and I, Buchanan sought to instil radical principles in his young charge, but provoked an opposite reaction.

Buchanan is a republican in the sense that the common-weal is his supreme political principle, making his views on limited constitutional monarchy far ahead of his time. Like many Protestant radicals, Buchanan develops the Biblical idea of a covenant or mutual pact between ruler and ruled. If this moral contract is broken then the ruler may be deposed. For the sixteenth century this was political dynamite and, in the seventeenth, the Scottish Covenanters pursued these principles at the cost of life and liberty, not least in Ayrshire.

However, unlike Knox and the Calvinist Covenanters, Buchanan emphasised the power of human conscience and free will as well as the corruption of human nature through sin. Both as historian and an esteemed national poet, Buchanan remained hugely influential in eighteenth-century Scotland, and his ideas are developed and acknowledged by both John Milton in his political essays and poetry and by the philosopher John Locke, both of whom were avidly read by Burns.

Locke's ideas were closely associated with the Revolution of 1688 which replaced James II and VII on the British throne with William of Orange and his spouse Mary. Paradoxically, Burns embraces this 'blow for liberty' while proclaiming the virtues of the consequently exiled Stewarts. But between these two positions is the Union of Scotland and England in 1707 which, for Burns, resulted in a loss of Scottish liberty and so a translation of the Old and Young Pretenders into symbols of national independence.

Locke espouses limited government and the concept of a social contract between ruler and ruled. Such contracts are to be guided by 'the law of God' which is also, for Locke, 'the law of reason' and the guarantor of morality. Locke, like Milton, is an advocate of religious tolerance, challenging the idea, common to Calvinists and Roman Catholic reformers, that monarchy along with one true religion were the joint pillars of social and political order. A religion of reason and conscience will contribute to human progress and improvement without the need for authoritarian regimes in Church or State. Cumulatively, these ideas formed Burns's political and religious views and they provide a consistent underpinning for his reactions to contemporary events.

In 1784 Robert penned a very specific ballad on the American War of Independence and its leading personalities 'When Guilford, Good'. Like many Scots, particularly the presbyterian modernisers, he sympathised with the struggle for independence. A full poetic treatment of this theme had to await the 'Ode for General Washington's Birthday' which was written in 1794.

> *No Spartan tube, no Attic shell,*
> *No lyre Æolian I awake.*
> *'Tis Liberty's bold note I swell:*
> *Thy harp, Columbia, let me take!*
> *See gathering thousands, while I sing,*
> *A broken chain, exulting, bring*
> *And dash it in a tyrant's face!*
> *And dare him to his very beard,*
> *And tell him he no more is fear'd,*
> *No more the despot of Columbia's race!*
> *A tyrant's proudest insults brav'd,*
> *They shout, a People freed! They hail an Empire sav'd!*[13]

By this time, Burns was in despair at the defeat of democratic reform in Britain, and the liberation of America contrasts with Caledonia's wild heaths from which freedom has fled. Interestingly, Andrew Noble and Patrick Scott Hogg, editors of *The Canongate Burns*, turned up an earlier version of the 'Ode' in which it is Hibernia's rather than Columbia's harp that the poet takes. This demonstrates Burns's sympathy with the democratic movement in Ireland which was to lead to the

[13] Henley, Vol. III, p. 195.

1798 rebellion. Burns, in turn, was celebrated by the United Irishmen and in particular the Presbyterian radicals.

The 'Address to Beelzebub' of 1786, again unpublished during the poet's lifetime, throws further light on Britain's relationship with the colonies. Burns reacts furiously to a news report of attempts by the Highland Society

> to frustrate the designs of Five hundred Highlanders who, as the Society were informed by Mr M'Kenna of Applecross, were so audacious as to attempt an escape from their lawful lords and masters whose property they were, by emigrating from the lands of Mr Macdonald of Glengary to the wilds of Canada, in search of that fantastic thing – Liberty.

The searing tone echoes Burns's most effective local satires.

Long Life, My Lord, an' health be yours,
Unskaith'd by hunger'd Highland boors!   unharmed
Lord grant, nae duddie, desp'rate beggar,   ragged
Wi' dirk, claymore, or rusty trigger
May twin auld Scotland o' a life,
She likes – as butchers like a knife!

Faith, you and Applecross were right
To keep the Highland hounds in sight!
I doubt na! they wad bid nae better   would
Than let them ance out owre the water;   over
Then up amang thae lakes an' seas   those
They'll mak what rules and laws they please.[14]

---

[14] Ibid., Vol. III, pp. 174–5, amended.

Framed painting of Robert Burns – full-length portrait by Alexander Nasmyth.
© Courtesy of the Trustees of Burns Monument and Burns Cottage.
Licensor www.scran.ac.uk

Burns Cottage, Alloway – the birthplace of Robert Burns, front view.
© Courtesy of the Trustees of Burns Monument and Burns Cottage.
Licensor www.scran.ac.uk

Miniature of Robert Burns, which belonged to Jean Armour Burns.
© Dumfries & Galloway Council – Nithsdale Museums.
Licensor www.scran.ac.uk

Jean Armour Burns. © Dumfries & Galloway Council – Nithsdale Museums.
Licensor www.scran.ac.uk

Edin.r Friday morning.

I cannot precisely say when I will leave this town, my dearest friend, but at farthest I think I will be with you on sunday come eight days, perhaps sooner. —— I had a horrid journey

I have settled matters greatly to my satisfaction with Mr Creech. — He is certainly not what he should be, and has given me what I should have, but I am better than I expected. — Farewel! I long much to see you — God bless you!

yours most sincerely

Robt Burns

Robert Burns house, Dumfries. © *The Scotsman Publications Ltd.*
Licensor www.scran.ac.uk

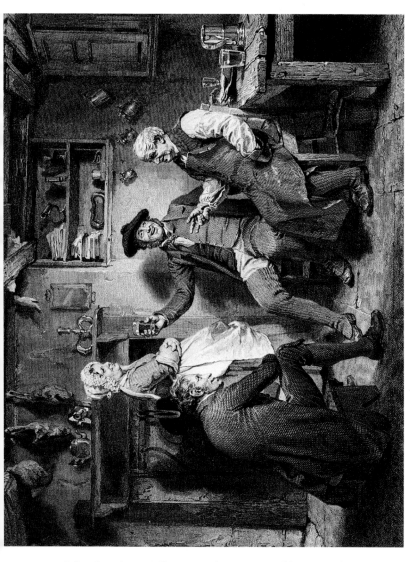

Robert Burns' 'Tam O'Shanter'. © The Scotsman Publications Ltd.
Licensor www.scran.ac.uk

Should auld acquaintance be forgot,
 And never brought to mind?
~~Should auld acquaintance be forgot,~~
 And days o' lang syne?
  Chorus
And for auld lang syne, my jo,
 For auld lang syne,
We'll tak a cup o' kindness yet,
 For auld lang syne.
And surely ye'll be your pint-stowp!
 And surely I'll be mine!
And we'll tak a cup o' kindness yet,
 For auld lang syne.
  And for &c.
We twa hae run about the braes,
 And pou'd the gowans fine;
But we've wander'd mony a weary foot
 Sin auld lang syne.
  And for &c.
We twa hae paidl'd i' the burn,
 Frae mornin sun till dine;
But seas between us braid hae roar'd,
 Sin auld lang syne.
  And for &c.
And there's a hand, my trusty fiere!
 And gie's a hand o' thine!
And we'll tak a right gude-willy waucht,
 For auld lang syne.
  And for &c.

However effective, the poem was unpublishable other than anonymously in a period when the Scottish aristocracy exercised unchallenged political and economic hegemony. This is Burns's bitter point in his squib 'The Creed of Poverty', written in response to a warning from the Excise Commissioners to keep out of politics.

In politics if thou wouldst mix
And mean thy fortunes be;
Bear this in mind, be deaf and blind,
Let great folks hear and see.[15]

However, when this sentiment was penned in 1795 Burns had already learned how to use the press to disseminate his political poetry anonymously or pseudonymously, just as his samizdat satires had circulated in Ayrshire in the 1780s.

The investigation into Burns's conduct by the Excise Commissioners, his government employers, arose from an incident in the Theatre Royal in Dumfries when the traditional singing of the national anthem was drowned out by calls for the revolutionary anthem 'Ça Ira'. The poet's defence was that he had neither initiated this *lèse-majesté* nor actively participated in it and that, moreover, he did not belong to any seditious group or association. In a letter to his Excise patron, Graham of Fintry, Burns insists that he is a defender of the British Constitution. This has been read by many commentators as craven submission to authority but, as Liam McIlvanney has recently pointed out, Burns means

---

[15] Ibid., Vol. IV, p. 32.

the constitution as established by the 'Glorious Revolution' of 1688 with its principles of social contract.[16] Even the Union of 1707 is governed by a 'covenant' based on the moral principles of mutual responsibility, respect and fairness.

The reproof dealt out by the Excise Commission thankfully fell short of dismissal, given Robert and his family were solely dependent on his salary. But this uncomfortable episode put a stop to Robert's more grand public gestures such as trying to send four impounded cannon to France or singing celebration ballads about France's victories in the pub. However, the flow of radical poems continued uninterrupted from 'On Glenriddel's Fox' to 'Here's a Health to Them That's Awa' and 'The Dagger'.

Nonetheless, the tide of events was turning because, as democratic clubs and societies sprang up all over Britain, the revolution in France shifted sharply from constitutional change to an all-out assault on the established order of Church, State and Monarchy. In May 1792 the British government banned Thomas Paine's 'Rights of Man' which was the brilliant democratic riposte to Edmund Burke's conservative 'Reflections on the Revolution in France'. Burns joins in with an outright claim for freedom of thought and expression.

Here's freedom to him that wad read,   would
Here's freedom to him that wad write!

---

[16] See Liam McIlvanney, *Burns the Radical: Poetry and Politics in Late Eighteenth Century Scotland* (East Linton: Tuckwell Press, 2002) passim, for the best recent account of Burns's politics and a defining account of the relationship between radicalism and Scottish Presbyterianism.

There's nane ever fear'd that the Truth should be heard,   none
But they whom the Truth wad indite.[17]

The next political poem that has been identified is an attack on Edmund Burke, published in *The Edinburgh Gazetteer* in May 1793 but which relates to an incident in the House of Commons the previous December. The poem is ascribed to 'Ane O' the Swine'. Burke had brandished a dagger asserting that the British radicals too would rise in bloody rebellion. There is a direct Dumfries connection here since the dagger in question was one of a consignment for which William Maxwell, a revolutionary sympathiser, was raising money to send to France. Maxwell was a Dumfriesshire landowner and Roman Catholic who had been a member of the Revolutionary Guard on the occasion of Louis XVI's execution, and who was later to become a friend of Burns as well as his doctor.

The illustrious Burke is given the same reductive treatment as Ayrshire ministers:

When a' the people thick an' thrang	busy
Disclose their minds sae fully,	
Permit me here to sing a sang	song
Of Paddy and his gully;	knife
(for Paddy's e'en a dainty chiel;	fellow
Glib gabbed an auld farran;	spoken / old-fashioned
An' can busk up a tale as weel	work up
As onie Lord or Baron)	any
I trow this day.	believe

[17] Henley, Vol. V, p. 270.

Had ye but seen him in his glee,
When he drew out his gully,
Ye maist wad swear that he should be,   most
The House o' Commons bully:
For when he's warmed in argument,
An' wants to be a bragger,
He handles weel the instrument   well
The all-convincing DAGGER,
On onie day.[18]

However, 'The Dagger' has a more subtle edge since the poet's point is that, though 'waving o' a gully' is a form of gesture politics, it introduces brute force into the heart of the political process. The reference to 'cannons' seems an indubitable pointer towards Burns as author, and his attempt to send four small guns to France.

But trouth I fear the Parliament
Its ancient splendour fully,
When chiels man back an argument   have to
By waving o' a gully:
Yet some there are, wi' honest heart,
(whose courage never swaggers)
Will ne'er the public cause desert,
For cannons or for daggers,
By night or day.[19]

---

[18] See Andrew Noble and Patrick Scott Hogg (eds), *The Canongate Burns* (Edinburgh: Scottish Classics, 2001), p. 456. We owe the recovery of this and other pseudonymous poems to Noble and Scott.

[19] Ibid., p. 457.

The poem finishes by praising the British Whigs and again asserting the Constitution as the guarantor of wellbeing for 'ilka British swain'.

In 1793 Burns was travelling in Kirkcudbrightshire and Dumfriesshire with his friend and fellow radical, John Sime. By chance at Annan they saw Thomas Muir being taken north under armed guard to stand trial for sedition. Muir, a lawyer and democrat, was the leading figure in the 'Friends of the People', the Scottish branch of the international radical movement. Muir was convicted of treason for membership of a banned association and for distributing Paine's outlawed 'Rights of Man'. Ironically, in sentencing Muir to fourteen years' transportation to Australia the Judge, Lord Braxfield, cited the perfection of the British Constitution which he asserted was incapable of improvement. The harshness of the sentences meted out to Thomas Muir and his earnest associates provoked widespread shock.

After the chance encounter with Muir, Robert went out for a walk, the tune 'Hey Tutti Tatti', which the Scottish troops were reputed to have sung on the march to Bannockburn, revolving in his mind. The result was 'Scots Wha Hae', a defiant anthem to liberty which links the historical and the contemporary struggle for freedom.

Lay the proud usurpers low
Tyrants fall in every foe
Liberty's in every blow
Let us do or die.[20]

---

[20] Henley, Vol. V, p. 150.

In 'Scots Wha Hae', poet and songmaker, radical and nationalist, democrat and patriot fuse in a way that continues to resonate in Scottish society.

At the time, however, the conviction of Muir was a terrible blow to the reforming cause, and Burns felt it personally and deeply. He continued to advocate democratic progress in poetry and prose, but he knew that the cause was stymied, not least by the outbreak of war between Britain and France. Yet this low point, aggravated by personal ill health and family worries, produced Burns's most remarkable testament of enduring faith in humanity, 'A Man's a Man For a' That'. When sending this poem to the song collector and editor, George Thomson, Robert described it diffidently as 'prose thoughts inverted into rhyme'. But the core strength of the composition is its harmonisation of abstract ideas into a universally understood melody.

'A Man's A Man' traces the now familiar development of Burns's political thought. The cottar of his early upbringing is once more the measure of integrity.

For a' that, an' a' that,
   Our toils obscure, an' a' that,
The rank is but the guinea's stamp,
   The man's the gowd for a' that.   gold

What though on hamely fare we dine,
   Wear hoddin grey, an' a' that?   coarse cloth
Gie fools their silks, and knaves their wine –   give
   A man's a man for a' that.[21]

[21] Ibid., Vol. V, p. 185.

The panoply of worldly rank and show cannot overturn the innate dignity and equality of human beings, which is expressed through intellectual sense and moral worth.

A Prince can mak a belted knight,
*   A marquis, duke, an' a' that!*
But an honest man's aboon his might –   above
*   Guid faith he mauna fa' that!*   must not grab
For a' that, an' a' that,
*   Their dignities, an' a' that,*
The pith o' sense and pride o' worth,
*   Are higher rank than a' that.*[22]

The last stanza is a prayer which combines Robert's Presbyterian inheritance with the ideals of liberty, equality and fraternity which he had imbibed, not from the French Revolution, but from the the Masonic Lodge.

Then let us pray that come it may,
*   As come it will for a' that,*
That sense and worth o'er a' the earth
*   Shall bear the gree an' a' that.*   be supreme
For a' that, an' a' that,
*   It's comin yet for a' that,*
That man to man the warld o'er
*   Shall brithers be for a' that.*[23]   brothers

'A Man's a Man' embodies a moment of resolution, belief and hope in the teeth of adversity. It unites politics and

[22] Ibid., Vol. V, p. 186.
[23] Ibid., Vol. V, pp. 186–7.

faith, ideas and feelings, in a way that has never been bettered.

The ideas of equality and respect ripple out across Burns's oeuvre, touching not just on democracy but on slavery, the rights of women, and the world of nature. Burns's relationships with women and the attitudes they reflect require a chapter to themselves, but the mature poet's vision of harmony is already explicit in the young farmer's 'To a Mouse' of November 1785, 'on turning her up in her nest with the plough'. Familiarity breeds contempt and every Scottish schoolchild has been compelled to readdress this unfortunate mouse. But Burns's poem remains a masterpiece 'for a' that'.

'To a Mouse' celebrates the bond of feeling between humanity and the animal world, which also symbolises proper relations between human beings. The poor oppressed mouse is like the wife of a small farmer turned out of her home or 'nest' by the arbitrary oppression of a landowner. Sympathetic feeling is the key to moral insight and unity but this is not the same as sentimentality.

In fact, there are cohesive philosophic ideas operating in 'To a Mouse'. First, there is Adam Smith's argument, familiar to Burns, that society cannot function without 'moral sentiments' qualifying and modifying the laws of economics. The key for Smith is sympathy generated by the mental habit of 'an impartial spectator' who sees the situation from different perspectives – in this case, those of the mouse and the ploughman. Nature intends humanity to be social but, without such an internalised moral sense, this is not possible. Yet, second, Burns also articulates a unity in nature reflecting the creation of man and animal by a benevolent and wise deity.

I'm truly sorry Man's dominion
Has broken Nature's social union,
An' justifies that ill opinion
         Which makes thee startle
At me, thy poor, earth-born companion
An' fellow-mortal.[24]

The mouse is not solely a metaphor for an oppressed fellow human being but also simply a mouse, just as the wounded hare Burns sees limping by is a suffering creature.

Inhuman man! curse on thy barb'rous art,
     And blasted be thy murder-aiming eye;
     May never pity soothe thee with a sigh,
Nor ever pleasure glad thy cruel heart!

Go live, poor wanderer of the wood and field,
     The bitter little that of life remains:
     No more the thickening brakes and verdant plains
To thee shall home, or food, or pastime yield.[25]

Implicit in a divinely created order is the desire for a more harmonious relationship between the natural and human worlds. That relationship, potential and actual, runs through Burns's poetry in a way that can only be described as ecological. In this regard, Burns's radicalism,

[24] Ibid., Vol. I, p. 256.
[25] Ibid., Vol. II, p. 219.

rooted in religion, anticipates twenty-first century ideas and challenges.

I doubt na, whyles, but thou may thieve;
What then? poor beastie, thou maun live!   must
A daimen icker in a thrave   ear in 24 sheaves
        'S a sma' request;
I'll get a blessin wi' the lave,   rest
        An' never miss't![26]

However, for Burns the touchstone of right thinking is always right feeling and, whatever judgement the impartial spectator may deliver, the bond between the participating actors should be one of compassion.

That wee bit heap o' leaves an' stibble,   stubble
Has cost thee monie a weary nibble!
Now thou's turned out, for a' thy trouble,
        But house or hald,   holding
To thole the Winter's sleety dribble,   bear
        An' cranreuch cauld![27]   hoar frost

Shared feeling is part of a sacred union of all nature. Yet compassion is also a distinctively human capacity and responsibility, since it is humanity that can look backwards and forwards, in hope and fear. Catastrophe comes on the poor fieldmouse as a bolt from the blue, but the special dignity of human beings lies in memory, foresight and free will. The ability to love is a heavenly gift.

[26] Ibid., Vol. I, p. 257.
[27] Ibid., Vol. I, p. 258.

Chapter Five

Love, Sex and Sin

In his youthful thirst for bookish learning Burns was untypical of an Ayrshire farmer's son. But in his sexual pursuits he was representative of his class and period. Writing to the novelist John Moore in 1787, between his Edinburgh sojourns, Robert detailed his first experience of love, contrasting it with the unremitting physical drudgery of the farm, and directly linking it with the impulse towards poetry and song.

This kind of life, the cheerless gloom of a hermit with the unceasing moil of a galley-slave, brought me to my sixteenth year; a little before which period I first committed the sin of rhyme. You know our country custom of coupling a man and woman together as Partners in the labours of Harvest. In my fifteenth autumn, my Partner was a bewitching creature who just counted an autumn less. My scarcity of English denies me the power of doing her justice in that language; but you know the Scotch idiom. She was a 'bonie, sweet, sonsie lass'. In short, she altogether unwittingly to herself initiated me in a certain delicious Passion, which in spite of acid Disappointment, gin-horse Prudence and bookworm Philosophy, I hold to be the first of human joys, our dearest pleasure here below. How she caught the contagion I can't say; you medical folks talk much of infection by breathing the same air, the touch, etc, but I never expressly told her that

I loved her. Indeed I did not well know myself why I liked her so much to loiter behind with her, when returning in the evening from our labours; why the tones of her voice made my heartstrings thrill like an Æolian harp; and particularly, why my pulse beat such a furious ratann when I looked and fingered over her hand, to pick out the nettle-stings and thistles. Among her other love-inspiring qualifications she sung sweetly; and 'twas her favourite reel to which I attempted giving an embodied vehicle in rhyme. I was not so presumptive as to imagine that I could make verses like printed ones, composed by men who had Greek and Latin; but my girl sung a song which was said to be composed by a small country laird's son, on one of his father's maids, with whom he was in love; and I saw no reason why I might not rhyme as well as he, for excepting smearing sheep and casting peats, his father living in the moors, he had no more Scholarcraft than I had.[1]

Retrospective though it is, this account has the freshness of immediate experience. And this freshness, along with its expression in song, becomes a model for poetic originality. Why depend on inherited tradition and convention when the poet can draw on the inspiration of the heart and senses? For Burns, this was an instinctive as well as a literary choice in which he anticipates Wordsworth and Coleridge. From this choice spring some of the greatest love songs in Scottish or English poetry.

It was upon a Lammas night,
    When corn rigs are bonie,   bonny

---

[1] W. E. Henley (ed.), *The Complete Writings of Robert Burns* (London: The Waverley Book Co., 1927), Vol. VII, pp. 8–9.

Beneath the moon's unclouded light,
I held awa to Annie;   made away
The time flew by, wi' tentless heed;
Till, 'tween the late and early,
Wi' sma' persuasion she agreed
To see me thro' the barley.

CHORUS
Corn rigs, an' barley rigs,
An' corn rigs are bonie:
I'll ne'er forget that happy night,
Amang the rigs wi Annie.   among

The sky was blue, the wind was still,
The moon was shining clearly;
I set her down, wi' right good will
Amang the rigs o' barley:
I ken't her heart was a' my ain;   all my own
I lov'd her most sincerely;
I kiss'd her owre and owre again,   over
Amang the rigs o' barley.[2]

The impact of these songs derives from the emotional strength, lyric simplicity and economy of expression, along with the natural setting. 'Corn Rigs' is a pre-harvest song of summer nights when the grain is heavy in the field rigs and the moon is full. Those who will labour together at the hairst are now free for a while to relax and roam into a world fruitfully at peace. There is an inherent promise of fertility and plenty.

[2] Ibid., Vol. II, pp. 46–7.

This mood and setting are also present in the August love song 'Westlin Winds'.

Now westlin winds and slaught'ring guns,
*   Bring Autumn's pleasant weather;*
The moorcock springs on whirring wings
*   Amang the blooming heather:*
Now waving grain, wide o'er the plain,
*   Delights the weary Farmer;*
The moon shines bright, as I rove at night,
*   To muse upon my Charmer.*[3]

The development of ideas is more complex in 'Westlin Winds' since the harmony of harvest love is contrasted with the violent dominion of the hunter, for whom the natural world is a source of prey and an arena of violent destruction.

Thus ev'ry kind their pleasure find,
*   The savage and the tender;*
Some social join, and leagues combine,
*   Some solitary wander:*
Avaunt, away, the cruel sway!
*   Tyrannic man's dominion!*
The sportsman's joy, the murd'ring cry,
*   The flutt'ring, gory pinion!*

But, Peggy dear, the ev'ning's clear,
*   Thick flies the skimming swallow,*

[3] Ibid., Vol. II, p. 49.

The sky is blue, the fields in view
  All fading-green and yellow:
Come let us stray our gladsome way,
  And view the charms o' Nature;
The rustling corn, the fruited thorn,
  And ilka happy creature.[4]   every

Love and love alone can restore the harmonious relationships
intended by the Creator. This is the road back to Eden. These
early love songs display extraordinary assurance for a young,
inexperienced poet. Burns has learned much from the Scots
song tradition but he is also remaking it by drawing directly
on his own experience.

In the long autobiographical letter to John Moore, Burns
mounts a retrospective defence of country love as a light-
hearted game, albeit one which provides the main enjoyment
of an otherwise labour-intensive lifestyle.

> At the plough, scythe or reap-hook I feared no competitor
> and set want at defiance: and as I never cared farther for
> my labours than while I was in actual exercise, I spent
> the evening in the way after my own heart – a country
> lad rarely carries on an amour without an assisting
> confidant – I possessed a curiosity, zeal and intrepid
> dexterity in these matters which recommended me a proper
> Second in duels of that kind; and I dare say, I felt as much
> pleasure at being in the secret of half the amours in the
> parish, as ever did Premier at knowing the intrigues of half
> the courts of Europe.

[4] Ibid., Vol. II, pp. 50–1.

The very goosefeather in my hand seems instinctively to know the well-worn path of my imagination, the favourite theme of my song; and is with difficulty restrained from giving you a couple of paragraphs on the amours of my compeers, the humble inmates of the farm-house and cottage; but the grave sons of science, ambition or avarice baptise these things by the name of follies. To the sons and daughters of labour and poverty they are matters of the most serious nature: to them, the ardent hope, the stolen interview, the tender farewell, are the greatest and most delicious part of their enjoyments.[5]

However, both the love songs and the autobiographical letter are carefully crafted artistic constructs. Is it possible to go behind the art and discern the relationships, sexual and otherwise, that formed Robert's attitudes?

Agnes Burnes, the poet's mother, is a shadowy figure in most accounts, though Catherine Carswell tries in her novelistic biography to breathe some life into this background yet surely important influence. Agnes kept to the traditional roles of a farmer's wife – housekeeping, child rearing and contributing to all the seasonal labour. However, she was a sociable person with a network of relations and friends; and her children were brought up in a strongly affirmative family atmosphere to which Robert remained emotionally attached all his life.

Agnes's piety was sincere and conventional but, in matters of public religion as in economic affairs, she deferred to her husband, upholding his principles through the family's many

[5] Ibid., Vol. VII, pp. 11–12.

struggles. Nonetheless, within her own household Agnes fostered the local traditional culture of song and story; all the supernatural and fairy lore of Ayrshire peasant tradition was passed on to her children. Agnes's cousin Betty Davidson was recognised as a keen storyteller while Agnes herself was a singer with an excellent memory and a repertoire of songs on which she drew for entertainment and education. The stories and the songs were part of the emotional bonding between adults and children, creating a warm, affectionate and encouraging environment.

Part and parcel of the household upbringing was physical intimacy and frankness about the processes of life and death on which every aspect of farming depended. The children were introduced from the beginning to songs about death, the troubles of life, and about its joys, including physical love. One of Agnes's songs which was a favourite with the children runs:

Kissin is the key o' love
An' clappin is the lock   cuddling
An' makin o's the best thing   of us
That e'er a young thing got.[6]   ever

Agnes Burness's approach to life seems to have been a blend of kind acceptance with fatalistic resignation. This is borne out by her attitude to the farm worker Lizzie Paton's relationship with Robert, and her willingness to bring up their baby when Lizzie refused to marry her son. It could be

[6] Catherine Carswell, *The Life of Robert Burns* (Edinburgh: Canongate Classics, 1990), p. 37.

argued, of course, that Robert her eldest was a favourite son who could do no wrong. But the evidence is of a practical woman who coped with life by caring for those around her whatever their origins or status. Through all the later complexities of his own relationships, Burns orientated his adult emotional life around a very similar woman, his wife Jean Armour.

However, as a young farm worker in Ayrshire, Robert's goal was full and free sexual relations between mutually attracted and consenting adults. This generally led to the birth of babies and either early marriages or a complex pattern of fosterage and informal adoption. Occasionally a tragedy might ensue with suicide or child murder as a result. It was not unknown for unwanted babies to be given to the travelling people or gypsies.

The Church waged a losing war against sex outwith marriage. The Kirk Sessions, composed of a small group of older males or 'elders', acted as a social court presided over by the minister. The same group was also legally responsible for poor relief and religiously responsible for charitable support. Kirk Session records reveal that the elders were often kindly and morally aware in the exercise of these responsibilities, but also that they could be severe and oppressive particularly towards women. The rules which Sessions enforced were designed to maintain social and economic order in a patriarchal land-owning society rather than bring in an ideal Christian order. Much depended on the lead given by individual ministers.

By the time Robert was growing up, however, the power of the minister and Session was on the wane. This was partly due to the growth of religious dissent but even more to economic change and the increased movement of population in search of work. William Burnes had left Kincardineshire (accompanied by a letter of recommendation from his minister) to go to Edinburgh and then Ayrshire. Subsequently he moved four times in Ayrshire, while his eldest son Robert nearly emigrated to Jamaica, spent time in Edinburgh and settled finally in Dumfries. William's younger son Gilbert moved after Robert's death from Ayrshire to East Lothian to work as a factor. The Kirk Sessions continued to define social respectability and were very influential on local society, but they could not strictly control such a mobile population.

When Lizzie's baby girl was born the Burnes family were still connected with Tarbolton Kirk under its liberal ministers, Patrick Woodrow and John McMath. There is no record of whether any disciplinary action was taken against Robert, though clearly the birth was a topic of scandal and gossip which would certainly have been reported to the Session. Robert seized the opportunity to assert his newly liberated values and build up his local reputation.

Thou's welcome, Wean! Mishanter fa' me,   child / misfortune fall
If thoughts o' thee, or yet thy Mamie,
Shall ever daunton me or awe me,
      My sweet, wee lady,
Or if I blush when thou shalt ca' me
      Tyta, or Daddie.   pet name

Tho' now they ca' me Fornicator,
An' tease my name in kintra clatter,   country gossip

The mair they talk, I'm kend the better;	more / known
E'en let them clash!	talk
An auld wife's tongue's a feckless matter	old / unsubstantial
To gie ane fash.[7]	any trouble

There is a strong element of bravado in these verses entitled 'A Poet's Welcome to his Love-begotten Daughter; the first instance that entitled him to the venerable appellation of Father'. Bravado becomes rebellious defiance in a song 'The Fornicator' written at the same time and sung to the aptly named traditional tune, 'Clout the Cauldron'.

Before the Congregation wide
   I pass'd the muster fairly,
My handsome Betsey by my side
   We gat our ditty rarely;   got / lesson
But my downcast eye by chance did spy
   What made my lips to water,
Those limbs so clean where I, between,
   Commenc'd a Fornicator.

With rueful face and signs of grace
   I pay'd the buttock-hire,
The night was dark and thro' the park
   I could not but convoy her;
A parting kiss, what could I less,
   My vows began to scatter,
My Betsey fell – lal de dal lal lal,
   I am a Fornicator.[8]

[7] Henley, Vol. III, pp. 3–4, amended.
[8] James Kinsley (ed.), *The Poems and Songs of Robert Burns*, Vol. I, p. 101.

Fornication was the formal charge which a Kirk Session would bring in such circumstances and, if found guilty, the culprits would sit at church 'on the cutty stool' and be publicly rebuked, perhaps on a series of Sundays. Maintenance of the child, through either marriage or other financial support from the father, would also be a concern of the Session.

Robert's appearance before the congregation as evoked in 'The Fornicator' may be more representative than actual, and this is borne out by the close relationship in style and tone between this song and the cantata 'Love and Liberty'. In fact, the caird or tinker's song in 'Love and Liberty' is appropriately set to the same tune, 'Clout the Cauldron'. Frank sensuality had become the expression of libertarian emotion and an attack on the hypocrisy and petty powers of a local social order. But both 'The Fornicator' and the cantata presume a social fellowship of defiance, and the limited capacity of the authorities to actually crack down on the sexual rebels. Defiance here is acted out rather than socially realised. Though neither of these works could be printed, they are less dangerous to the author in local terms than the direct attack on an elder's sexual misdemeanours in 'Holy Willie's Prayer'.

The use of sexual bawdy as a language of liberty became strongly established in Burns's poetry. His songs of sexual licence, 'The Merry Muses of Caledonia', were written for male friends and sung at social gatherings in the taverns and at the private clubs in which Burns delighted, including the Tarbolton Bachelors and the Crochallan Fencibles in Edinburgh. They are sexual hymns to liberty and not to be confused with libertinism. Throughout, the artist remains in control, not least in 'Love and Liberty' which is a technically accomplished masterpiece.

Burns was to ruefully acknowledge the relative security of his earlier position in his autobiographical letter, when he recounted how a further love affair brought him within firing range of the Mauchline Kirk Session, including William Fisher. This was a more serious conflict with direct consequences for Burns and Jean Armour, the new focus for his passion. Jean's pregnancy did result in Burns appearing in public at church in Mauchline to be rebuked. But this was no ordinary disciplinary routine applied to a wayward country couple. Rev. William Auld was the champion of the Calvinist Puritans and Robert a noted critic and satirist of the Mauchline Kirk Session and its minister. Moreover, Burns was closely identified with Gavin Hamilton who was arch-enemy number one as far as the Calvinist faction was concerned.

On a personal level too, this conflict was deeper and more dangerous than anything the young poet had previously experienced. Robert and Jean were wholeheartedly in love and committed to marriage. In traditional style they had 'plighted their troth' to each other, and Robert had written out a marriage agreement which both had signed. By Scots law they were legally married but Jean's father, James Armour, contemptuously destroyed the document leading Burns to mistakenly believe that Jean had betrayed him. He felt both emotionally devastated and humiliated.

But worse was to come. James Armour was a firm supporter of Auld and the Kirk Session. Acting probably with their collusion, he took out a civil action against Robert seeking financial damages and support for his daughter. Had this action been successful the lease for Mossgiel, which was in the names of Robert and Gilbert, would have been lost to provide ready money, leaving the whole Burnes family homeless. Fortunately, Gavin Hamilton who was then Burns's landlord, got wind of this action and helped Robert defend it. But he also orchestrated the precaution by which the lease was signed over to Gilbert. This was the point at which Robert resolved to emigrate to the West Indies.

During this difficult period, Burns maintained his poetic defiance in satires such as 'Libel Summons' in which a series of Mauchline's young eligibles, including the poet, are called to account for their sexual misdemeanours. The 'Summons' attacks the hypocrisy of the ecclesiastical court but also outs those who have been unwilling to take responsibility for the results of their 'houghmagandie'.

This fourth o June, at Mauchline given,
The year 'tween eighty five and seven,
We, Fornicators by profession,
As per extractum from each Session,
In way and manner here narrated,
Pro bono Amor congregated;
And by our brethren constituted,
A Court of Equity deputed –
With special authoris'd direction
To take beneath our strict protection,
The stays-out-bursting, quondam maiden,
With Growing Life and anguish laden;

Who by the rascal is deny'd,
That led her thoughtless steps aside. –
He who disowns the ruin'd Fair-one,
And for her wants and woes cares none;
The wretch that can refuse subsistence,
To those whom he has given existence;
He who when at lass's by-job,   vagina
Defrauds her wi a frig or dry-bob;   petting / no climax
The coof that stands on clishmaclavers   fool / nonsense
When women halfins offer favours: halfway
All who in any way or manner
Disdain the Fornicator's honour,
We take congisance thereanent,
The proper Judges competent.[9]

The culprits are arraigned by name and those who are brother Masons receive an especial condemnation.

The 'Summons' has some of the buoyancy of Robert's earlier 'Welcome' to Lizzie Paton's daughter, but his satire 'Adam Armour's Prayer', also written during these months, is darker in tone. A local prostitute attached to Poosie Nancy's Tavern had been attacked by a group of Mauchline men including Jean's brother Adam and dragged through the streets in a barbaric medieval style punishment, possibly for carrying venereal disease. Burns's bitter poem puts these words into young Armour's mouth:

Gude, pity me because I'm little,
For though I am an elf o' mettle,

[9] Ibid., Vol. I, pp. 256–7, amended.

And can, like ony wabster's shuttle, weaver's
  Jink there or here; dodge
Yet, scarce as lang's a guid kail whittle, good cabbage knife
  I'm unco queer.

An' now Thou kens our woefu' case, knows
For Geordie's Jurr we're in disgrace, maid
Because we stang'd her through the place, rode on a pole
  An' hurt her spleuchan, purse / vagina
For which we daurna show our face
  Within the clachan.[10] village

Armour and his friends have been charged with assault for this incident and he is praying for various lowlife Mauchline characters, including George Gibson the landlord, to be tortured in hell. But 'Geordie's Jurr' is ironically to be spared and, in a deft twist, Burns emphasises the brutal sexist treatment which had been meted out.

As for the Jurr, puir worthless body! – poor
She's got mischief enough already;
Wi' stanget hips and buttocks bluidy, wounded
  She's suffered sair;
But may she wintle in a woodie, spin on the gallows
  If she whore mair![11] more

This was not a happy period for Robert and he experienced both guilt and depression.

---

[10] Henley, Vol. III, pp. 15–16.
[11] Ibid., Vol. III, p. 17.

Oh enviable early days,
When dancing thoughtless pleasure's maze,
*   To care, to guilt unknown!*
How ill exchang'd for riper times,
To feel the follies, or the crimes,
*   Of others, of my own!*[12]

In a series of poetic farewells Burns articulated his decision to leave Scotland. In addition to his personal troubles, Robert was publicly attacked for immorality by a rhyming tailor, Thomas Walker, who turned the poet's favoured form, the Verse Epistle, against him. In riposte, Robert produced a new version of his disputed appearance before the Kirk Session.

This leads me on to tell for sport,
How I did wi' the Session sort:
Auld Clinkum at the inner port   bellringer / gate
*   Cried three times, 'Robin!'*
'Come hither lad and answer for't,
*   Ye're blam'd for jobbin'.*   fornication

Wi' pinch I put a Sunday's face on,
An' snoov'd awa' before the Session.   tripped off
I made an open, fair confession. –
*   I scorn'd to lie –*
An' syne Mess John, beyond expression,   then Master
*   Fell foul o' me.*

---

[12] Ibid., Vol. I, p. 275.

A fornicator lown he call'd me,   loon
An' said my faut frae bliss expell'd me;   fault from
I own'd the tale was true he tell'd me,
 'But what the matter,'
Quo' I, 'I fear unless ye geld me,   castrate
 I'll ne'er be better!'

'Geld you!' quo' he, 'an' what for no,
If that your right hand, leg, or toe,
Should ever prove your spr'tual foe,
 You should remember
To cut it aff, and what for no,
 Your dearest member?'

'Na, na' quo' I, 'I'm no for that,
Gelding's nae better than 'tis ca't,   is called
I'd rather suffer for my faut,
 A hearty flewit,   flogging
As sair owre hip as ye can draw't,   sore over
 Tho' I should rue it.

Or gin ye like to end the bother,
To please us a', I've just ae ither,   one other
When next wi' yon lass I foregather,
 Whate'er betide it,
I'll frankly gie her 't a' thegither,   give / all together
 An' let her guide it.'[13]

Burns rewrites his clash with authority as an act of reversal, pouring scorn on his judges and deploying obscenity to

[13] Ibid., Vol. III, pp. 91–3.

upturn their sexual repression. The defiance and satire are still there but the harsh tones mitigate against the poet's better feelings as much as the benighted tailor.

In reality, Robert's feelings were more complex and divided than this account has so far suggested. While pursuing his heartfelt affair with Jean Armour, and sincerely aiming at marriage, Robert also harboured the notion of a relationship with a more sophisticated educated woman, who would kindle other aspects of his poetic being. A number of different candidates for this role were considered, the principal being Peggy Chalmers who was related to Gavin Hamilton and often at her father's house in Mauchline. Timing is complex in this period, despite James Mackay's heroic efforts to accurately plot the course of events in his biography of the poet. But at some point during the Jean Armour romance, Robert also became interested in Mairead Campbell, a Highlander whom he first met as a servant in Gavin Hamilton's house and later saw when she moved to become a dairymaid at the Montgomery estate at Coilsfield.

As the Jean Armour relationship hit the premarital rocks, the Campbell relationship hotted up to the point at which she and Burns swore faithfulness to each other on Mairead's Bible and agreed to meet in Greenock on the eve of Robert's departure for the New World. No part of Burns's life has been more romanticised than the 'Highland Mary' (she was really a 'Margaret') of his love songs; but Mackay also points to significant evidence that Mairead Campbell was already sexually experienced and conducting a liaison with Colonel Montgomery's cousin Lord Eglinton. This is not proof of some personal moral turpitude on Mairead's part, but illustrative of the vulnerability of female farm workers to sexual exploitation. Nonetheless, it does throw a different light on Burns's own relationship with Mairead and her subsequent death in Greenock. The suggestion that Mairead Campbell was pregnant is not borne out by any firm evidence, but it seems likely that Burns's relationship with 'Highland Mary' was sexually consummated.

Robert's personal circumstances had moved a long distance from the innocent passions of his early love songs, well before the sudden success of the *Kilmarnock Edition* and his impulsive decision to head for Edinburgh late in 1786. From the perspective of 1786 it could be fairly argued that he was the victim of unusual circumstances. But the patterns that emerged in 1786 were to recur in Edinburgh and again in Dumfries.

Burns aspired to marriage as a loving relationship which combined sexual union with stimulating companionship. But what society seemed to offer the young farmer was either an intellectual exchange with a woman removed from the possibility of both sexual relations and marriage by reasons of class, or sexual intimacy with an amiable but uneducated woman of Burns's own social class. He felt this divide keenly because his artistic aspirations reached beyond his immediate social environment and his education, or self-education, had given the young poet a clear sense of other possibilities. Simultaneously, Burns felt the pull of sexual passions unconstrained by either social or intellectual conventions. Add to this the economic pressures on Robert's choices, depressive tendencies, and the needs of his widowed mother, siblings and an infant daughter, and the instabilities of this emergent artist become all too apparent.

Yet some of these pressures were of Robert's own making; his craving for new and sometimes contradictory experiences seems to derive as much from his psychology as from his circumstances. A measure of internal conflict may have derived from parental influences. While Agnes Brown's warm and intimate nurturing made Burns physically confident and at ease with himself, William Burnes's ideals were based on physical self-control and repression in favour of mental or spiritual aspirations.

From the beginning Robert was hungry for new experiences, and relationships were the means by which he explored identities and possibilities. The young poet's life energies were motivated, perhaps driven, by a hungry curiosity which, given his constrained social and educational circumstances, sought release by every available means. Inevitably, insecurity fuelled this hunger for new experience, physical, emotional and intellectual. In addition, underlying heart problems deriving from hard physical work at too early a stage of development may have contributed their own cycle of exhilaration and depression.

At points in his twenties these pressures threatened to overwhelm Burns. On his return from Irvine, and again after his rejection by the Armours, he felt that he was losing his sanity. More specifically, Robert describes this as the loss of rational guidance – the centrality of reason which had been at the core of his father's instruction and his own drive for self-improvement. Reason might be overrun by depressed spirits undermining thought or motivation, or by an outbreak of 'folly' by which Burns meant chaotic indulgence – the gratification of impulse on all sides without balance or discrimination.

Self-confessed 'folly' and 'melancholy' haunt Burns's poetry and prose from young adulthood to maturity and death. The last poem in the *Kilmarnock Edition* of July 1786 is a sober reflection on the recent crisis months, cast as an epitaph on the deceased poet.

Is there a whim-inspired fool,
Owre fast for thought, owre hot for rule,   over
Owre blate to seek, owre proud to snool? –   shy / grovel
      Let him draw near;
And owre this grassy heap sing dool,   lament
And drap a tear.[14]   drop

At twenty-seven years of age Burns exhibits considerable self-knowledge.

Is there a man whose judgement clear
Can others teach the course to steer,
Yet runs, himself, life's mad career
      Wild as the wave? –
Here pause – and, thro' the starting tear
      Survey this grave.

The poor Inhabitant below
Was quick to learn and wise to know,
And keenly felt the friendly glow
      And softer flame;

14 Ibid., Vol. II, p. 65.

But thoughtless follies laid him low,
    And stain'd his name.[15]

This is retrospective but also prescient since self-knowledge is no guarantee of changed behaviour. As St Paul uncomfortably reflected in words with which Robert was familiar, 'the good that I would, I do not; the evil I would not, that I do' (Romans 7:15).

In the letter to Moore, Burns places emphasis on his quest for self-knowledge and describes vividly how his relationships were his means of self-measurement.

> It is ever my opinion that the great, unhappy mistakes and blunders, both in a rational and religious point of view, of which we are thousands daily guilty, are owing to their ignorance, or mistaken notions of themselves. To know myself had been all along my constant study. I weighed myself alone, I balanced myself with others; I watched every means of information how much ground I occupied both as a Man and as a Poet; I studied assiduously Nature's Design where she seem'd to have intended the various *lights* and *shades* in my character. I was pretty sure my Poems would meet with some applause, but at the worst, the roar of the Atlantic would deafen the voice of Censure and the novelty of West-Indian scenes make me forget Neglect.[16]

However, for Burns the cross-currents of self-awareness and emotional compulsion meet in his relations with women. The prospect of a permanent attachment seemed to

[15] Ibid., Vol. II, pp. 65–6.
[16] Ibid., Vol. VII, p. 17.

provoke a reactive lunge towards some other object of desire. Sometimes, when a distant object came too close, Burns felt an immediate need to transfer emotional allegiance to a more inaccessible figure. A relationship which demanded sensitive emotional and social handling could push Robert towards instant sexual gratification. This is a different more specific aspect of the chaos which Burns acknowledged. Contrary desires could be simultaneously pursued with sometimes destructive – including self-destructive – results.

Such complex and chaotic situations were not consciously intended on Burns's part. In the 'Epistle to a Young Friend', he counsels against sexual licence and deceit while acknowledging that 'mankind are unco weak / An' little to be trusted':

The sacred lowe o' weel placed love,	glow
Luxuriantly indulge it;	
But never tempt th' illicit rove,	
Tho' naething should divulge it:	nothing
I waive the quantum o' the sin,	
The hazard of concealing;	
But, och! it hardens a' within,	all
And petrifies the feeling![17]	

This is surely wise advice yet, interestingly, Burns also counsels the young friend to 'still keep something to yourself / Ye scarcely tell to any'. This was advice that Robert himself followed so well in his relations with Mairead Campbell that

[17] Ibid., Vol. I, p. 294.

we are still essentially in the dark. Then, during his second stay in Edinburgh in 1787–8, Burns became involved in another sexual tangle about which we are considerably better informed.

When Robert returned to Edinburgh in October 1787 from his self-publicising tours of Scotland, he was in love with Peggy Chalmers with whom he had finally struck up a friendship, both in Edinburgh and at the Harvieston estate beneath the Ochil Hills in Clackmannanshire. There he asked her to marry him but she refused while insisting on remaining friends. Peggy gave no reason for her refusal but she was already secretly engaged to a young banker, Lewis Hay. For the same reason she asked Burns not to publish the songs he had written about her at Harvieston.

Lacking the true explanation, Robert must have bitterly concluded that Peggy Chalmers had declined marriage on the basis of his class. This was aggravating to Burns's wounded pride since, to all appearances, he had been accepted as an equal at Harvieston and participated fully in the social activities as both a young guest of spirit and a respected poet. Worse, Peggy's refusal seemed to derail Robert's aspirations towards a marriage of minds and sensibilities which transcended Ayrshire and the messy course of his relations with Jean Armour.

Back in Edinburgh, Burns continued to correspond with Peggy and to treat her as a close friend who understood his better nature. After meeting Agnes, or Nancy, McLehose and beginning their long correspondence, Burns refers to 'the first of women' whose 'name is indelibly written in my heart'. Nancy is quick to spot that this cannot be Jean

Armour without guessing the 'fair one's' identity. Later, when the relationship with the epistolary 'Clarinda' was running its course, Burns lent Peggy's letters to Nancy to read, ostensibly to demonstrate his friend's worth. In reality Robert is exhibiting his capacity for cultured friendship with women, at a point when Nancy remains sceptical on this very issue.

The element of gamesmanship persists through the correspondence, more perhaps on Sylvander's part than Clarinda's. The truth is that the friendship was very risky for Nancy McLehose, threatening her good name and perhaps the vital support extended to her by a small network of friends and relations. Although Nancy was effectively a deserted wife, responsible for two young sons, she had technically initiated separation from the alcoholic and depressive James McLehose. Her parents were both dead and her status in respectable society vulnerable.

Despite these factors, Burns entered willingly into extended correspondence and enthusiastically into a subsequent series of face-to-face assignations. This was because Nancy McLehose offered not just a replacement for Peggy Chalmers, but a relationship that went much further in terms of role playing and emotional experiment. Spurned by Peggy and confined for weeks by an injury to his knee, Robert was in every way ready for a new romantic attachment.

The cult of sensibility or fine emotion was closely connected in the late eighteenth century with a Scottish novel, *The Man of Feeling*, by Burns's literary patron, Henry Mackenzie. Both Robert and Nancy were enthusiastic devotees, and her aim was to develop a literary friendship in which emotional attachment would blend with mutual artistic exchanges – a correspondence of poets. Robert indulged this desire and acknowledged Nancy as a woman of intelligence and taste who had, moreover, suffered appalling treatment at the hands of those from whom she had the right to expect protection and respect.

However, as the letters flew between Robert's lodging in St James Square and Nancy's flat in Potterrow, his sexual interests were aroused and, when Sylvander and Clarinda met, he began a series of attempts to seduce this very attractive young mother who had experienced life in all its emotional ups and downs. Nancy fought hard to maintain her original idea of a relationship that provided intellectual adventure and emotional fulfilment in an otherwise fairly restricted existence. But inevitably she was drawn in more deeply than intended and passions were stirred. Nancy was now playing with fire. Robert was acutely sympathetic to her predicament, tied to a man whom she could not love while denied the love of a true soul mate. Such sympathies, though, only fed the flames of frustrated desire. At one level, both parties revelled in the emotional indulgence. At another, serious consequences were to ensue for both Sylvander and Clarinda.

Throughout the whole short-lived affair between Robert and Nancy there was a vital middle term in the relationship – religion. In his opening letters, Burns outlines the mutual sympathy that should bind two such sensitive and talented individuals in their respective struggles with life. But, for Robert, such sympathy naturally informs the tender passions especially when one of the parties is 'a gloriously amiable fine woman'. Nancy firmly reminds him that she is married and not 'some vain silly woman to make a fool of her – or worse'. Robert ripostes that 'there is no holding converse ... without some mixture of that delicious passion, whose most devoted slave I have, more than once, had the honour of being'. He then expostulates on his theme.

> But why be hurt or offended on that account? Can no honest man have a prepossession for a fine woman, but he must run his head against an intrigue? Take a little of the tender witchcraft of love, and add it to the generous, the honourable sentiments of any friendship, and I know but one more delightful morsel, which few, few in rank ever taste. Such a composition is like adding cream to strawberries: it not only gives the fruit a more elegant richness, but has a peculiar deliciousness of its own.[18]

The argument here, which Clarinda will repudiate, is that friendship between men and women is not possible without sexual attraction. This is clearly based on Burns's own experience in which, from his viewpoint, women are either needing care and protection as the 'weaker' sex or objects of desire, or both. Nancy McLehose, however, holds out for a different understanding of the relationship between love and friendship.

> I believe there is no friendship between people of sentiment and of different sexes, without a *little* softness; but when kept within proper bounds, it only serves to give a higher relish to such intercourse. Love and Friendship are names

[18] Ibid., Vol. X, p. 12

in every one's mouth; but few, extremely few, understand their meaning. Love (or affection) cannot be genuine if it hesitate a moment to sacrifice every selfish gratification to the happiness of its object. On the contrary, when it would purchase *that* at the expense of *this*, it deserves to be styled, not love, but by a name too gross to mention. Therefore, I contend, that an honest man *may* have a friendly prepossession for a woman, whose soul would abhor the idea of an intrigue with her. These are my sentiments upon this subject: I hope they correspond with yours.[19]

This is feminism in the making but of a very specifically eighteenth-century variety. Women of taste and sentiment should be free to engage in friendships and cultural exchanges but protected by Christian virtue rather than a contemporary understanding of rights. Nancy McLehose is a strong example of the Enlightenment influence in Scotland where religion, education and culture come together in an improving and virtuous harmony. Another of Burns's correspondents, Elizabeth Rose of Kilravock, has left us a careful record of her reading and reflections in a series of commonplace books. In an original study of these fascinating and little understood sources, Mark Towsey comes to a series of conclusions which are applicable to the younger and less affluent Mrs McLehose.

> Though on the face of it compliant and entirely respectful of the authority of the printed word, Elizabeth's reading was actually highly selective and original, and she wilfully imposed her own religious, moral and political values on

[19] Ibid., Vol. X, pp. 17–18.

readings that did not entirely match them. She identified and transcribed the single passages in Smith's *Moral Sentiments* and Beattie's *Elements of Moral Science* that she considered most relevant to her own situation, and ransacked other books for material that would help her understand the most pressing problems in her life. Above all it is evident that Elizabeth Rose approached the books she owned or borrowed from friends and neighbours with a distinct view of the ends of reading and learning. For this woman, reading was a virtuous occupation that was explicitly intended to effect her own moral improvement – to prepare her for the world of action into which she had suddenly been thrust in 1782, to prepare her to be a dutiful landholder, a virtuous mother, a responsible educator, an attentive reader and a sympathetic friend. In the process, she illuminated the world of the female reader in Scotland in an age of Enlightenment and demonstrated that even women could engage in the foremost intellectual debates of the age.[20]

The question to be asked is: did Burns fully comprehend where such women were coming from? In his case the list includes Peggy Chalmers, Nancy McLehose and later a rather different personality, the aristocratic Maria Riddell who was young, beautiful and perhaps more open to a frankly sexual relationship. Defenders of Burns's egalitarian philosophy can claim the 'Rights of Woman' prologue which he wrote for the young (and beautiful) actress Louise Fontenelle. However,

[20] Mark Towsey, 'An Infant Son to Truth Engage: Virtue, Responsibility and Self-Improvement in the Reading of Elizabeth Rose of Kilmarnock, 1747–1815', in *The Journal of the Edinburgh Bibliographical Society* Number Two (2007), pp. 85–6.

despite its daring reference to the French Revolution anthem 'Ça Ira', this poem upholds the stereotype of women as needing protection and love. In the light of what we know about his own relationships, Burns's emphasis on decorum and the eighteenth-century equivalent of a 'new man' has a theatrical quality.

> *First, in the Sexes' intermix'd connexion,*
> *One sacred Right of Woman is Protection*
> *The tender flower, that lifts its head elate,*
> *Helpless, must fall before the blasts of fate,*
> *Sunk on the earth, defac'd its lovely form,*
> *Unless your Shelter ward th' impending storm.*
>
> *Our second Right – but needless here is caution –*
> *To keep that Right inviolate's the fashion:*
> *Each man of sense has it so full before him,*
> *He'd die before he'd wrong it – 'tis Decorum!*
> *There was, indeed, in far less polish'd days,*
> *A time, when rough, rude Man had naughty ways:*
> *Would swagger, swear, get drunk, kick up a riot,*
> *Nay, even thus invade a lady's quiet!*
> *Now, thank our stars! these Gothic times are fled;*
> *Now, well-bred men – and you are all well-bred –*
> *Most justly think (and we are much the gainers)*
> *Such conduct neither spirit, wit, nor manners.*[21]

Robert's outlook is more fully revealed in an onslaught on Nancy's reservations and reserve. By this point, the

[21] Henley, Vol. III, pp. 169–70.

correspondents had completely assumed their pastoral pen names 'Sylvander' and 'Clarinda'.

> 'Tis true I never saw you but once: but how much acquaintance did I form with you at that once! Do not think I flatter you, or have a design upon you, Clarinda: I have too much pride for the one, and too little cold contrivance for the other; but of all God's creatures I ever could approach in the beaten way of acquaintance, you struck me with the deepest, the strongest, the most permanent impression. I say the most permanent, because I know myself well and how far I can promise either on my prepossessions or powers. Why are you unhappy? And why are so many of our fellow-creatures, unworthy to belong to the same species with you, blest with all they can wish? You have a hand all-benevolent to give; why were you denied the pleasure? You have a heart formed, gloriously formed, for all the most refined luxuries of love; why was that heart ever wrung? O Clarinda! shall we not meet in a state, some yet unknown state of being, where the lavish hand of Plenty shall minister to the highest wish of Benevolence; and where the chill north-wind of Prudence shall never blow over the flowery fields of Enjoyment? If we do not, man was made in vain! I deserved most of the unhappy hours that have lingered over my head; they were the wages of my labour; but what unprovoked demon, malignant as hell, stole upon the confidence of unmistrusting, busy fate, and dashed your cup of life with undeserved sorrow?[22]

Robert's assault is based on religious principles, namely the intentions of a benevolent Creator for his creatures, male and female. These provide a context for loving relationships

[22] Ibid., Vol. X, pp. 12–13.

and for the fulfilment of individual lives. Yet even Burns in full flow has to admit that there are blockages on the road to freedom. Unhappiness and its frustration are the product of unworthy fellow humans or even 'a malignant demon'. A similar mixed picture applies to Burns himself as he freely admits to Clarinda.

> I don't know if you have a just idea of my character, but I wish you to see me as *I am*. I am, as most people of my trade are, a strange Will-o'-wisp being; the victim, too frequently, of much imprudence, and many follies. My great constituent elements are *pride and passion*: the first I have endeavoured to humanise into integrity and honour; the last makes me a devotee, to the warmest degree of enthusiasm, in love, religion, or friendship – either of them, or altogether, as I happen to be inspired.[23]

The giveaway or warning note for Nancy is the 'either of them, or altogether, as I happen to be inspired'! For Robert, all can be merged and forgiven in the afflatus of emotion. Far from being reassured by Burns's theological perspective, Clarinda detects irreligion and responds with her own understanding of the relationship between un-happiness and faith. Only an adherence to moral virtue can repel the true unhappiness of guilt and sin. All else may be endured and even turned into a schooling in virtue and sympathy.

> Take care: many a 'Glorious' woman has been undone by having her head turned. 'Know *you*!' I know *you* far better

[23] Ibid., Vol. X, p. 12.

than you do me. Like yourself, I am a bit of an enthusiast. In Religion and Friendship quite a Bigot – perhaps I could be so in Love too; but everything *dear to me* in heaven and earth forbids! This is my fixed principle; and the person who would dare to endeavour to remove it I would hold as my chief enemy. Like you, I am incapable of *Dissimulation*; nor am I, as you suppose, unhappy. I have been unfortunate; but guilt alone could make me unhappy. Possessed of fine Children, – Competence, Fame, Friends, kind and attentive – what a monster of ingratitude should I be in the eye of Heaven were I to style myself unhappy! True, I have met with scenes too *horrible* for recollection – even at six years' distance; but adversity, my Friend, is allowed to be the school of virtue. It oft confers that chastened softness which is unknown among the favourites of Fortune! Even a mind possessed of natural sensibility, without this, never feels that exquisite pleasure which nature has annexed to our sympathetic sorrows. Religion, the only refuge of the unfortunate, has been my balm in every woe. O! could I make Her appear to you as she has done to me! Instead of ridiculing her tenets, you would fall down and worship her very semblance wherever you found it![24]

This makes Robert fully aware of what he is up against, a convinced and considered religious believer. The correspondence is now threatening to become more about theology than love so Sylvander refutes the charge of irreligion – 'Your religious sentiments, Madam, I revere' – and restates his own core philosophy of charity, while moving the dialogue back onto his own favoured ground.

[24] Ibid., Vol. X, pp. 14–15.

My definition of Worth is short: Truth and Humanity respecting our fellow-creatures; Reverence and Humility in the presence of that Being, my Creator and Preserver, and who, I have every reason to believe, will one day be my Judge. The first part of my definition is the creature of unbiased Instinct; the last is the child of after Reflection. Where I found those two essentials, I would gently note and slightly mention any attendant flaws – flaws, the marks, the consequences of Human nature.

I can easily enter into the sublime pleasures that your strong imagination and keen sensibility must derive from Religion, particularly if a little in the shade of misfortune; but I own I cannot, without a marked grudge, see Heaven totally engross so amiable, so charming a woman as my friend Clarinda; and should be very well pleased at a circumstance that would put it in the power of Somebody, happy Somebody! to divide her attention, with all the delicacy and tenderness of an earthly attachment.[25]

This reorientation is vital to Burns as his first visit to Nancy McLehose is now scheduled for the next evening. On that visit Robert leaves a version of his life story, the autobiographical letter, with his hostess to read at her leisure. What will the reaction be to his (mainly) honest and open account of life and loves?

Burns did not have to wait long, and Nancy's first reactions are highly promising.

I cannot delay thanking you for the packet of Saturday; twice have I read it with close attention. Some parts of it did beguile me of my tears. With Desdemona, I felt 'twas pitiful,

[25] Ibid., Vol. X, pp. 22–3.

'twas wond'rous pitiful'. When I reached the paragraph where Lord Glencairn is mentioned, I burst out into tears. 'Twas that delightful swell of the heart which arises from a combination of the most pleasurable feelings. Nothing is so binding to a generous mind as placing confidence in it. I have ever felt it so. You seem to have known this feature in my character intuitively; and, therefore, instructed me with all your faults and follies. The description of your first love-scene delighted me. It recalled the idea of some tender circumstances which happened to myself at the same period of life – only mine did not go so far. Perhaps, in return, I'll tell you the particulars when we meet.[26]

This is how men and women of feeling are to engage and commune! Then came the sticking point: 'One thing alone hurt me, though I regretted many – your avowal of being an enemy of Calvinism.' The following passages in Clarinda's letter are reminiscent of a Muslim woman insisting that her wearing of the veil is a personal choice and positive expression of identity and not a symbol of oppression. Nancy describes how she was educated in the modernising traditions of Presbyterianism but chose Calvinist belief as an adult in Edinburgh through the influence of the Tron Kirk minister, Rev. John Kemp, and her own investigations: 'conviction of understanding, and peace of mind, were the happy consequences'.[27]

The convictions to which Nancy refers are, in summary, humanity's condition of sin through the fall of Adam, the

[26] Ibid., Vol. X, pp. 26–7.
[27] Ibid., Vol. X, p. 28.

need for divine salvation through Jesus Christ, the sacrifice on the cross which closes the gap between God's righteousness and human sinfulness, and the sequence of repentance, forgiveness and sanctification by which individuals can participate in the life of God through Christ. This, Clarinda insists, is not cold rationalistic religion, nor does it repress our humanity, but it does require specific faith in Jesus Christ as God's Son.

> I intended to resume a little upon your favourite topic, the 'Religion of the bosom'. Did you ever imagine that I meant any other? Poor were that religion and unprofitable whose seat was merely in the brain. In most points we seem to agree: only I found all my hopes of pardon and acceptance with Heaven upon the merit of Christ's atonement – whereas you do upon a good life. You think 'it helps weel, at least'. If anything we could do had been able to atone for the violation of God's Law, where was the need (I speak it with reverence) of such an astonishing Sacrifice? Job was an 'upright man'. In the dark season of adversity, when other sins were brought to his remembrance, he boasted of his integrity; but no sooner did God reveal Himself to him, than he exclaims: 'Behold I am vile, and abhor myself in dust and ashes.' Ah! my friend, 'tis pride that hinders us from embracing Jesus we would be our own Saviour, and scorn to be indebted even to the 'Son of the Most High'. But this is the only sure foundation of our hopes. It is said by God Himself, ''tis to some a stumbling block: to others foolishness' but they who believe feel it to be the 'Wisdom of God and the Power of God'.[28]

---

[28] Ibid., Vol. X, p. 42.

Clarinda's creed could fairly be described as mainstream Protestantism, and excludes what she calls the 'dark tenets' of Calvinism, such as predestination or a belief in the total degradation of humanity.

Some of this Burns could agree with, but he was also careful to restate things in his own way, even quoting the Bible in the manner of the Protestant moderniser. First of all, Robert shies away from the implication that those who do not undergo the due Calvinist process of salvation will suffer judgement and punishment. The benevolent Creator is compassionate above all and 'is not willing that any should perish but that all should come to eternal life'. Free will is essential to this wise design since otherwise how could human beings have a fair and equal chance of embracing the good? Rather than suffering divine judgement 'the deceiving and uncharitable' exclude themselves from eternal bliss 'by their unfitness for enjoying it'.

To the Calvinist, this is soft religion which does not address the harsh realities of the human condition, and Nancy McLehose had seen much in her own experience that confirmed a bleaker view. Moreover, for Nancy, Burns was unreliably vague on the status and person of Jesus Christ, which was the cohering centre of Calvinist belief. For Robert, Jesus Christ is 'a great Personage' whose relation to God we cannot comprehend but whose relation to humanity is as 'Guide and Saviour'. In less guarded theological moments Burns described Jesus as more of a brother and a friend than a saviour. For Calvinists, this was moving towards 'deism', the general belief in a Supreme Being rather than the specific belief in God's once and for all act of salvation in Jesus Christ, 'His only Son'.

Clarinda was very aware that intense theological debate might become a turn-off, however avid the pair's desire for intellectual companionship. She realised, she wrote, that Burns would be either laughing, yawning or reaching for the theology text books. And anyway, this strenuous philosophising was giving her a headache. She therefore reverted to some firm marital counselling:

> You told me you never had met with a woman who could love as ardently as yourself. I believe it; and would advise you never to tie yourself, till you meet with such a one. Alas you'll find many who *canna*, and some who *manna*, but to be joined to one of the former description would make you miserable. I think you had almost best resolve against wedlock; for unless a woman were qualified for the companion, the friend, and the mistress, she would not do for you.[29]

Who could possibly meet such a triple requirement? If only she were not already married.

From this juncture, the correspondence between Sylvander and Clarinda lurched into a growing emotional imbroglio between Robert and Nancy. As their face-to-face encounters increased, her Calvinist self-restraint wobbled. A pattern emerged in which she would be carried further than she intended or desired, and then draw back in a retrospective mélange of guilt and recrimination. However, the further she moved, the less it was enough for Robert,

[29] Ibid., Vol. X, p. 29.

who found the two steps forward two back rhythm galling and frustrating.

But on Robert's side of this relationship there was a brewing yet undecided crisis. During the previous summer on a visit to Mauchline, Burns had administered sexual comfort to the abandoned, yet still welcoming, Jean Armour. She was now once again pregnant and her father, outraged by this further extramarital misdemeanour, had thrown her out of the family home in the depths of winter. Serious poverty and exposure now threatened.

At one level, Robert knew that his time in Edinburgh was drawing to a close. The crisis in Ayrshire was effectively his family crisis and he would have to return and address it. Marriage to Jean Armour loomed. Behind the scenes he was feverishly considering his options: taking a lease on another farm with his remaining literary earnings as capital or securing a commission as an Excise Officer. In due course he achieved both but this was far from certain in January 1788. Moreover, Robert was stuck in Edinburgh trying repeatedly, but unsuccessfully, to extract his earnings from the *Edinburgh Edition* of his poetry out of the publisher, William Creech.

Characteristically, Burns's reaction to these cumulative pressures was chaotic. As the Clarinda melodrama wound on without tangible result, Robert began an affair with Nancy McLehose's maid, Jenny Clow. Whether Burns simply applied his charms casually in pursuit of sexual relief or whether Jenny decided to upstage her mistress is unclear, but a liaison began. Jenny lodged in the Cowgate where many working- class girls existed in a twilight zone between city living and outright prostitution. Burns was well acquainted with this demi-monde and Jenny was not the only working-class girl with whom he had casual sexual relations during his Edinburgh sojourns.

Whether the Jenny Clow affair was entirely casual, or even a subconscious act of revenge on Clarinda, is unknown but it did result in a pregnancy which would prove especially galling to Burns. First of all, Nancy's discovery of Jenny's condition, after Robert had left Edinburgh, resulted in bitter recriminations and a shattering of the carefully constructed illusion that Clarinda and Sylvander were still united in an eternal meeting of minds and hearts. Later again it was Nancy who had to inform Burns, now safely married to Jean in Dumfriesshire, of Jenny's illness and poverty. Robert travelled to Edinburgh to make amends but, even on her deathbed in the Cowgate, poor Jenny refused to give her infant son to his natural father. The young Robert Burns was adopted by an elderly childless couple, and grew up to have a successful career in the East India Company.

As all of this was simmering, still in prospect, Nancy's situation became perilously exposed. She and Burns had begun to exist in a bubble of their own making, but Edinburgh was not a private environment. Several of Nancy's close female friends knew of the relationship, while Robert had openly flaunted the affair with his friend, Robert Ainslie, even introducing him to Clarinda. Both of the key figures in Nancy McLehose's support network, her minister and spiritual counsellor Rev. John Kemp and her cousin and financial prop William Craig, got wind of the Burns connection and came down hard on their dependent protégé. Nothing could be more threatening to respectable Edinburgh than a questionable relationship with the controversial 'rustic' poet. Furthermore, according to both Nancy and Robert, William Craig had his own more than cousinly intentions towards Clarinda.

The fat was in the fire and a sequence of events in both Ayrshire and Edinburgh now hastened the passionate yet unconsummated affair to a close. Both partners milked the coda emotionally, yet both knew that things had run their course and were privately relieved.

In retrospect, Nancy's view was that both he and she had transgressed the bounds of propriety, but more importantly they had sinned by indulging their passions instead of observing the restraints of Christian love. Robert's view was the opposite: they had sinned against the law of life by not following the impulses of heart and body. Nature had designed them to be united by love.

But Burns's position is contradictory, since by 'the law of life' he was also the father of Jean Armour's unborn twins while clandestinely indulging in a sexual liaison with Jenny Clow and perhaps other vulnerable working-class women. This does not match up to Burns's 'religion of the bosom', the higher moral law of the heart. It is more like a chaotic surrender to contending impulses. For Nancy McLehose this was sin and required repentance. For Robert it was folly tinged with dissipation, and deserving of the compassionate understanding of a God who had created humanity with feelings and desires. What it meant to Jenny Clow is neither known nor much considered.

Inconsistency is, of course, a human failing. It is understandable that, in almost alternate breaths, Burns could be praising the moral influence of Henry Mackenzie's novels on a rakish friend, and boasting to another laddish mate about two game young women he had fallen in with on his travels. But, at points of crisis in his life, Robert was capable of a surrender to impulse that imposed hurt on those about him and threatened to undermine, rather than enhance, key relationships. The Jean–Nancy–Jenny triangle was not the first of Burns's making and, even when settled in Dumfries with a growing family, he managed to have a tempestuous on–off relationship with the upper-class Maria Riddell while also fathering a baby with a young barmaid at the Globe Inn. Like Agnes Brown before her, Jean Armour took the new baby under her wing like one of her own. Rob, she laconically commented, needed more than one wife. In return, Jean received some incomparable love songs and this husbandly summing-up conveyed, at the beginning of the marriage, to Peggy Chalmers.

> Shortly after my last return to Ayrshire, I married 'my Jean'. This was not in consequence of the attachment of romance perhaps; but I had a long and much loved fellow-creature's happiness or misery in my determination, and I durst not trifle with so important a deposit. Nor have I any cause to repent it. If I have not got polite tattle, modish manners, and fashionable dress, I am not sickened and disgusted with the multiform curse of boarding-school affectation; and I have got the handsomest figure, the sweetest temper, the soundest constitution, and the kindest heart in the country.[30]

[30] Ibid., Vol. VIII, p. 80.

Chapter Six

Life, Death and the Devil

It would be easy to conclude from Burns's Edinburgh adventures that he was a man fatally divided against himself. This would be wrong. It is also possible to construct a picture of Burns as a flawed romantic genius, doomed to a tragic fate from which he wrested great art. This would also be mistaken. Even the depiction of Burns as primarily an artist of Romantic emotion is off the mark.

Burns believed that humanity was endowed with gifts of reason and feeling and that these could, and should, be brought into harmony with each other. He did not accept Hume's analysis that 'reason is, and ought only to be, the slave of the passions',[1] any more than he adopted Hume's supposed atheism. Equally, he repudiated the Calvinist analysis of humanity helplessly beset by sin; and he attacked all institutional structures, political or religious, which were based on asserting the innate inequality or inadequacy of human beings. People, Burns believed, had been created by a benevolent deity to achieve happiness; and the natural world, reason and our better emotions all supported that view, despite the hardships to which life is prone.

[1] David Hume, *A Treatise of Human Nature* (1739), Bk 2, Part 3, Section 3.

In the eighteenth century such a philosophy was described as deism, and it would not be inaccurate to describe Burns as a Christian deist or deistic Christian. One could also map out the link between Burns and the Enlightenment philosophers including Locke, Rousseau, Voltaire and Adam Smith as well as the common sense of Thomas Reid and Dugald Stewart. Although Burns absorbed these writers' ideas he was no systematic philosopher, and it may be more helpful to think of Burns as being in the Wisdom tradition, which reaches from the ancient world, through Jewish and Christian scriptures, to the Christian Humanists such as Rabelais, Erasmus, George Buchanan, Montaigne and Cervantes, and then, through Alexander Pope, to the Sterne of *Tristram Shandy*.

These writers are united by a religious faith which inspires the humane virtues, ridicules while also celebrating human folly, and excoriates unjust oppression. Their natural languages are poetry and imaginative prose, rather than scholastic rationalism. They seek enlightenment but not at the expense of humanity, and are therefore sceptical of ideologies and utopias. Burns's immediate literary forebears, Allan Ramsay and Robert Fergusson, belong to the same broad European stream.

One of Robert's early moral satires, 'Address to the Unco Guid', begins with a very accomplished Scots paraphrase from the Biblical book of Ecclesiastes which is a fundamental text of Jewish Wisdom.

My son, these maxims make a rule,
An' lump them ay thegither: together

The Rigid Righteous is a fool,
The Rigid Wise anither;
The cleanest corn that e'er was dight   winnowed
May hae some pyles o' caff in;   grains of chaff
So ne'er a fellow-creature slight   never
For random fits o' daffin.   merry folly

Solomon (Eccles. 7:16)[2]

The poem proceeds to expound the play in human life of Wisdom and Folly, to advocate charity and mercy as the fruits of Wisdom, and to undermine the complacency and hypocrisy of the well-doing and unco guid.

O Ye wha are sae guid yoursel,   good
Sae pious and sae holy,
Ye've nought to do but mark and tell
Your neebours' fauts and folly;   neighbours' faults
Whase life is like a weel-gaun mill,   smoothly turning
Supplied wi' store o' water;
The heapet happer's ebbing still,   heaped hopper
An' still the clap plays clatter!   clapper

Hear me, ye venerable Core,
As counsel for poor mortals,
That frequent pass douce Wisdom's door
For glaikit Folly's portals;   daft
I, for their thoughtless, careless sakes,
Would here propone defences –

[2] W. E. Henley (ed.), *The Complete Writings of Robert Burns* (London: The Waverley Book Co., 1927), Vol. II, p. 108.

Their donsie tricks, their black mistakes,   unlucky
      Their failings and mischances.

Ye see your state wi' theirs compared,
      And shudder at the niffer,   comparison
But cast a moment's fair regard,
      What makes the mighty differ?
Discount what scant occasion gave,
      That purity ye pride in;
And (what's aft mair than a' the lave)   more / rest
      Your better art o' hidin.[3]

This is building up to the often quoted, familiar admonition:

Then gently scan your brother Man,
      Still gentler sister Woman;
Tho' they may gang a kenning wrang,   least thing wrong
      To step aside is human:
One point must still be greatly dark,
      The moving why they do it;
And just as lamely can ye mark,
      How far perhaps they rue it.[4]

Andrew Noble and Patrick Scott Hogg, editors of *The Canongate Burns*, link this directly with Robert's first Commonplace Book, in particular the following passage:

  I have often observed in the course of my experience of human life that every man even the worst, have something

[3] Ibid., Vol. II, pp. 108–9.
[4] Ibid., Vol. II, pp. 110–11.

good about them … Let any of the strictest character for regularity of conduct among us, examine impartially how many vices he has never been guilty of, not from any care or vigilance, but from want of opportunity or some accidental circumstance intervening; how many of the weakness's of mankind he has escaped because he was out of the line of such temptation; and what often, if not always, weighs more than all the rest, how much he is indebted to the World's good opinion, because the world does not know all; I say any man who can thus think, will scan the failings, nay the faults and crimes of mankind around him, with a brother's eye.[5]

This is interesting because of the way in which it shows the young Burns developing this thought in parallel prose and poetry. In the same Commonplace Book, Robert praises Adam Smith's *The Theory of Moral Sentiments*.

I entirely agree with that judicious Philosopher Mr Smith in his excellent Theory of Moral Sentiments, that Remorse is the most painful sentiment that can embitter the human bosom. Any ordinary pitch of fortitude may bear up tolerably well under those calamities, in the procurement of which we ourselves have had no hand; but when our own follies or crimes have made us miserable and wretched, to bear it up with manly firmness, and at the same time have a proper penitential sense of our misconduct – is a glorious effort of Self-command.[6]

The conclusion is particularly significant: guilt and penitence demonstrate moral self-improvement and self-control,

5 Ibid., Vol. VII, p. 253.
6 Ibid., Vol. VII, p. 251.

rather than the influence of a God who, according to the seventeenth- and eighteenth-century Calvinists, demands repentance before conferring forgiveness. Here in 1783, at the start of his adult maturity, Robert is carving out his own personal philosophy. He was not to know that Luther, Calvin and Knox had actually put the grace, or initiative, of God first before anything else, though he would have also disliked their giving human free will second place. This prose reflection is linked with a fragmentary exercise of Robert's in dramatic blank verse entitled 'Remorse'.

Of all the numerous ills that hurt our peace;
That press the soul, or wring the mind with anguish;
Beyond comparison the worst are those
That to our Folly, or our Guilt we owe.
In ev'ry other circumstance the mind
Has this to say, 'it was no deed of mine'.
But, when to all the evil of misfortune
This sting is added, 'blame thy foolish self';
Or worser far, the pangs of keen remorse:
The torturing, gnawing consciousness of guilt –
Of guilt, perhaps where we've involved others;
The young, the innocent, who fondly lov'd us;
Nay more, that very love their cause of ruin!
O! burning Hell! in all thy store of torments
There's not a keener lash!
Lives there a man so firm who, while his heart
Feels all the bitter horrors of his crime,
Can reason down its agonising throbs,
And, after proper purpose of amendment,

Can firmly force his jarring thoughts to peace?
O happy, happy, enviable man!
O glorious magnanimity of soul![7]

To absorb such self-inflicted wounds, to make amends, and to move on is the purpose of humanity, not to fall back into pessimism and misanthropy.

This emphasis on moral improvement or development is shared by Burns with the key moral philosophers of the Scottish Enlightenment. These include James Beattie, Professor of Moral Philosophy at Aberdeen University, whose poetry Robert admired; and Dugald Stewart, who held the same position at Edinburgh University while remaining close to his roots in Ayrshire society. Burns came to know Stewart personally and penned this portrait of the genial, virtuous philosopher in his second Commonplace Book, most of which was written in Edinburgh.

> The most perfect character I ever saw is Mr Stewart. An exalted judge of the human heart, and of composition. One of the very first public speakers; and equally capable of generosity as humanity. His principal discriminating feature is – from a mixture of benevolence, strength of mind and manly dignity, he not only at heart values but, in his deportment and address, bears himself to all the actors, high and low, in the drama of life, simply as they merit in playing their parts. Wealth, honours, and all that is extraneous of the man, have no more influence with him than they will have at the Last Day. His wit, in the hour of social hilarity, proceeds

[7] Ibid., Vol. III, pp. 288–9, amended.

almost to good-natured waggishness; and in telling a story he particularly excels.[8]

Burns is still at work fashioning ideas and observations in prose as well as poetry, with the unifying aim of understanding human nature in all its variety. This pursuit brings him close to Elizabeth Rose and Nancy McLehose, in their cultivation of virtue in reading and writing.

Throughout his life, letter writing continued to be Robert's vehicle for exploring his ideas in the context of his relationships, and it is in letters that he feels moved or, in some cases, compelled to sum up his views on life and religion. This was a frequent theme in correspondence with his older female friend and advisor, Mrs Dunlop, who is another in the school of Elizabeth Rose and Clarinda, requiring reassurance on Robert's Christian convictions.

That there is an incomprehensibly Great Being, to whom I owe my existence, and that he must be intimately acquainted with the operations and progress of the internal machinery, and consequent outward deportment of this creature which he has made; these are, I think, self-evident propositions ... I will go further and affirm that, from the sublimity, excellence and purity of his doctrine and precepts unparalleled by all the aggregated wisdom and learning of many preceding ages, though to *appearance*, he himself was the obscurest and most illiterate of our species; therefore Jesus Christ was from God.[9]

[8] Ibid, Vol. VII, p. 142.
[9] Ibid., Vol. VIII, p. 194.

These serious affirmations are, however, prefaced – stimulated in fact – by Burns's reactions to that morning's sermon delivered at Dunscore Parish Church, near Ellistand, by the Rev. Joseph Kirkpatrick.

> I have just heard Mr Kirkpatrick give a sermon. He is a man famous for his benevolence and I revere him; but from such ideas of my Creator, good Lord deliver me![10]

A more relaxed letter to his close male friend, Alexander Cunningham, explicitly places illiberal religion in the realm of human folly, along with class prejudice and snobbery.

> But of all Nonsense, religious nonsense is the most nonsensical; so enough and more than enough of it. Only, by the bye, will you, or can you tell me, my dear Cunningham, why a religious turn of mind has always had a tendency to narrow and illiberalize the heart? They are orderly; they may be just; nay, I have known them merciful: but still your children of Sanctity move among their fellow creatures with a nostril snuffing putrescence, and a foot spurning filth – in short, with that conceited dignity which your titled Douglases, Hamiltons, Gordons, or any other of your Scots Lordlings of seven centuries standing, display when they accidentally mix among the many-aproned Sons of Mechanical life.[11]

This is revealing because it demonstrates that Burns's primary quarrel with the unco guid is not a theological disagreement but one caused by their offences against moral wisdom and human fellowship.

[10] Ibid., Vol. VIII, p. 194.
[11] Ibid., Vol. IX, pp. 91–2.

In Wisdom thinking ideas, especially religious ideas, function with exactly this relational or existential quality. On the eve of the extended crisis of 1786–7 Burns writes to Robert Aiken, another close male friend, of his own religious feelings at this time.

> You may perhaps think it an extravagant fancy, but it is a sentiment which strikes home to my very soul; though sceptical, in some points, of our current belief, yet, I think, I have every evidence for the reality of a life beyond the stinted bourne of our present existence: if so, then, how should I, in the presence of that tremendous Being, the Author of existence, how should I meet the reproaches of those who stand to me in the dear relation of children, whom I deserted in the smiling innocency of helpless infancy? O thou unknown Power! thou Almighty God! who has lighted up reason in my breast and blessed me with immortality! I have frequently wandered from that order and regularity necessary for the perfection of thy works, yet thou hast never left me nor forsaken me![12]

To read this is to understand that, through all the Edinburgh experiments, an unbroken thread connected Robert to what, like his father, he regarded as the most important human ties.

More moving, if not more heartfelt or sincere, is Robert's letter in 1788 to his old friend Robert Muir in Kilmarnock from whom, as a young man in trouble, he had often received hospitality, advice and help. Muir was now seriously ill.

[12] Ibid., Vol. VII, p. 81.

I trust the spring will renew your shattered frame and make your friends happy. You and I have often argued that life is no great blessing on the whole. The close of life indeed, to a reasoning eye, is

> Dark as was chaos, ere the infant sun
> Was roll'd together, or had try'd his beams
>   Athwhart the gloom profound.

But an honest man has nothing to fear. If we lie down in the grave, the whole man a piece of broke machinery, to moulder with the clods of the valley – be it so; at least there is an end of pain, care, woes and wants: if that part of us called Mind does survive the apparent destruction of the man – away with old-wife prejudices and tales! Every age and every nation has had a different set of stories; and, as the many are always weak of consequence, they have often, perhaps always, been deceived: a man, conscious of having acted an honest part among his fellow creatures – even granting that he may have been the sport, at times, of passions and instincts – he goes to a great unknown Being, who could have no other end in giving him existence but to make him happy; who gave him those passions and instincts, and well knows their force.

These, my worthy friend, are my ideas; and I know they are not far different from yours. – It becomes a man of sense to think of himself; particularly in a case where all men are equally interested, and where indeed all men are equally in the dark.[13]

This constitutes a more radical expression of Robert's beliefs, comparing religious versions of an after-life to a set of stories and even to 'old-wife prejudices and tales'. The admission

[13] Ibid., Vol. VIII, pp. 21–2.

of darkness, chaos and death strikes a pessimistic note, characteristic of Wisdom literature such as the Book of Ecclesiastes. Yet this is counterbalanced by faith in a merciful divine being who will ensure that, whatever death brings, it will not be arbitrary or cruel. Even oblivion may be kindly. This is faith as understood between men of 'sense' and radical convictions. Yet, it is expressed in a specific letter of comfort and consolation. Muir died within a month of receiving the letter.

In another letter to Mrs Dunlop, written in 1795, Burns sums up his religion of humanity and wisdom.

> With all my follies of youth and, I fear, a few vices of manhood, still I congratulate myself on having had in early days religion strongly imprinted on my mind. I have nothing to say to any body as to which sect they belong, or what creed they believe; but I look on the man who is firmly persuaded of Infinite Wisdom and Goodness superintending and directing every circumstance that can happen in his lot. I felicitate such a man as having a solid foundation for his mental enjoyment; a firm prop and sure stay in the hour of difficulty, trouble and distress; and a never-failing anchor of hope, when he looks beyond the grave.[14]

Once again, this underpins the consistency of Robert's views throughout his adult life. It is, however, also the pronouncement of a settled married man and father to a growing family, who led household prayers as William Burnes had done before him, and attended St Michael's Parish Kirk in

[14] Ibid., Vol. IX, p. 216.

Dumfries on Sundays in a spirit of social responsibility and solidarity, as well as reverence to that which is greater than the individual human self.

However, to practise wisdom is to also appreciate folly and this is where the Devil enters Burns's equation, mainly as a figure of fun. One of the sparkling early satires is 'Address to the Deil' which appeared in the *Kilmarnock Edition*. The target and therefore the fun of the poem is doubled because, in addressing 'O thou whatever title suit thee – Auld Hornie, Satan, Nick, or Clootie –', Burns is revelling in country superstition and assaulting a central pillar of Puritan belief. After all, without the Devil, where are the torments of Hell? The poet himself acknowledges the importance of this infernal Being.

Great is thy pow'r an' great thy fame;	
Far kend, an' noted is thy name;	known
An' tho' yon lowan heugh's thy hame,	burning pit
Thou travels far;	
An' faith! thou's neither lag, nor lame	behindhand
Nor blate nor scaur.	shy / afraid
Whyles, ranging like a roarin lion,	
For prey, a' holes an' corners tryin.	all
Whyles, on the strong-wing'd Tempest flyin,	
Tirlan the kirks;	unroofing
Whyles, in the human bosom pryin,	
Unseen thou lurks.[15]	

---

[15] Ibid., Vol. I, pp. 177–8.

The poet's authority for this knowledge turns out to be his 'rev'rend Graunie' who is well-informed about Auld Nick, both through traditional lore and personal experience.

I've heard my rev'rend Graunie say,
In lanely glens ye like to stray;
Or where auld ruin'd castles grey
           Nod to the moon,
Ye fright the nightly wand'rers way
           Wi' eldritch croon.   unearthly

When twilight did my Graunie summon,
To say her pray'rs, douce, honest woman!   decent
Aft yont the dyke she's heard you bummin,   beyond the wall
           Wi' eerie drone;
Or, rustlin, thro' the boortries coman,   elder trees
           Wi' heavy groan.[16]

There are loud echoes here of Robert's own experience and his reception, through his mother's older cousin Betty Davidson, who was 'remarkable for her ignorance, credulity and superstition', of 'the largest collection in the county of tales and songs concerning devils, ghosts, fairies, brownies, witches, warlocks, spunkies, kelpies, elf-candles, dead-lights, wraiths, apparitions, cantraips, giants, inchanted towers, dragons and other trumpery'.[17]

In an interesting essay, 'Burns and Superstition', Professor Ted Cowan suspects Burns of over-identifying with the

[16] Ibid., Vol. I, p. 178.
[17] Ibid., Vol. VII, pp. 5–6.

Enlightenment disdain for popular traditions.[18] After all, this was the culture of the folk rather than the intellectual or landed elite. However, that is to abstract Robert from his own Enlightenment roots. As Cowan describes, Burns remained ambivalent about folk traditions even when devoted to the collection of popular songs and music, but he knew their poetic power and acknowledged their influence in his autobiographical letter to Dr Moore.

> This cultivated the latent seeds of Poesy; but had so strong an effect on my imagination, that to this hour in my nocturnal rambles I sometimes keep a sharp look-out in suspicious places; and though nobody can be more sceptical in these matters than I, yet it often takes an effort of Philosophy to shake off these idle terrors.[19]

In 'Address to the Deil' the poet admits to a humorous personal encounter.

Ae dreary, windy, winter night,	
The stars shot down wi' sklentin light,	slanting
Wi' you myself, I gat a fright:	got
Ayont the lough,	
Ye, like a rash-buss, stood in sight,	rush bush
Wi' waving sugh:	sough
The cudgel in my nieve did shake,	fist
Each bristl'd hair stood like a stake;	

[18] See Edward J. Cowan, 'Burns and Superstition', in Kenneth Simpson (ed.), *Love and Liberty; Robert Burns: A Bicentenary Celebration* (East Lothian: Tuckwell Press, 1997), pp. 229–38.

[19] Henley, Vol. VII, p. 6.

When wi' an eldritch, stoor 'quaick, quaick',	deep
Amang the springs,	among
Awa he squatter'd like a drake,	took noisy flight
On whistling wings.[20]	

The 'Address' proceeds to describe various devilish manifestations in warlocks, witches, curses, water kelpies, deluding lights or spunkies, and even the raising of the Devil himself through misuse of Masonic secrets. But the summit or origin of all devilish mischief is the Fall of Man.

Lang syne in Eden's bonie yard,	long since / bonny
When youthfu' lovers first were pair'd,	
An' all the soul of love they shar'd,	
The raptur'd hour,	
Sweet on the fragrant flow'ry swaird,	sward
In shady bow'r.	

Then you, ye auld, snick-drawing dog!	latch loosing
Ye cam to Paradise incog,	
An' played on man a cursed brogue	trick
(Black be your fa'!)	fall
An' gied the infant warld a shog,	shake
'Maist ruin'd a'.[21]	almost

There is no more devastating assault on the core of Puritan belief in eighteenth-century literature. The Fall, and humanity's consequent degradation, is the pillar of

---

[20] Ibid., Vol. I, pp. 178–9.
[21] Ibid., Vol. I, pp. 181–2.

Calvinism; Burns's rumbustiously reductive humour was meant, and taken, as a deadly affront. For the godly it was outright proof of Robert's irreligion, since to deny the Devil was tantamount to atheism.

However, educated Presbyterian as he was, Burns is able to use the Bible for his own purposes and the Address goes on to cite the Devil's attempt to undermine the Old Testament faith of Job.

D'ye mind that day when in a bizz	bustle
Wi' reeket duds, an' reestet gizz,	smoky clothes / burnt wig
Ye did present your smoutie phiz	dirty face
'Mang better folk;	among
An' sklented on the man of Uzz	squinted
Your spitefu' joke?	

An' how ye gat him i' your thrall,	got
An' brak him out o' house an' hal',	break
While scabs an' blotches did him gall,	
Wi' bitter claw;	
An' lows'd his ill-tongu'd wicked scaul –	loosed / scolding wife
Was warst ava?[22]	worst of all

The Book of Job has a framing story in which God dispatches Satan to test Job, and the unknown author uses the story like a traditional myth in order to provide poetic context for his drama of questioning and faith. The Book of Job, like Ecclesiastes, is a prominent example of ancient Wisdom literature.

[22] Ibid., Vol. I, p. 182.

Burns, however, has moved beyond the Biblical author of Job by putting the Calvinist Puritan icon of the Devil on the same level as the irrational beliefs of illiterate peasants, as this letter to Alexander Cunningham conveys, albeit written with the help of a bottle of Antigua Rum.

O, thou Spirit! whatever thou art, or wherever thou makest thyself visible! Be thou a Bogle by the eerie side of an auld thorn, in the dreary glen through which the herd-callan maun bicker in his gloaming route frae the fauld! Be thou a brownie, set, at dead of night, to thy task by the blazing ingle, or in the solitary barn, where the repercussions of thy iron flail half-affright thyself, as thou performest the work of twenty of the sons of men, ere the cock-crowing summon thee to thy ample cog of substantial brose! Be thou a kelpie, haunting the ford, or ferry, in the starless night, mixing thy laughing yell with the howling of the storm and the roaring of the flood, as thou viewest the perils and miseries of Man on the foundering horse, or in the tumbling boat! Or, lastly be thou a ghost, paying thy nocturnal visits to the hoary ruins of decayed Grandeur, or performing thy mystic rites in the shadow of the time-worn church while the moon looks, without a cloud, on the silent, ghastly dwellings of the dead around thee; or taking thy stand by the bed-side of the Villain, or the Murderer, portraying, on his dreaming fancy, pictures, dreadful as the horrors of unveiled Hell, and terrible as the wrath of incensed Deity! Come, thou spirit![23]

The Devil had become, in Robert's hands, a literary device deployed for comic or satiric effect, in the same way as

[23] Ibid., Vol. IX, pp. 89–90.

Death appears with his rusty scythe in 'Death and Doctor Hornbook'. But there are still distinctions to be drawn. The Beelzebub of Robert's political invective 'Address of Beelzebub' is a deadly serious mouthpiece for aristocratic oppression and disdain. Neither is the Devil of the 'Address' the same Satan whom Burns admires as the hero of Milton's *Paradise Lost*, though his youthful satire does make a glancing reference to St Michael driving the rebellious prince of darkness from heaven. Robert had to defend his admiration for Milton's Satan to Clarinda.

> My favourite feature in Milton's Satan is his manly fortitude in supporting what cannot be remedied: in short, the wild broken fragments of a noble exalted mind in ruins. I meant no more by saying he was a favourite hero of mine.[24]

This is, of course, ingenuous since, for Burns, Milton's Satan is a Prometheus, and he anticipates many later critics in establishing him as the true hero of the epic.

Nonetheless, by common consent the Devil's star appearance in Burns's own work is in the complex comic masterpiece 'Tam O' Shanter'. The catalyst for this late poem was the antiquarian peregrinations of Captain Francis Grose. The Riddells of Friars Carse, who were supporters of Burns and neighbours when he and Jean lived at Ellisland, entertained Grose and introduced him to the poet. In return, Robert provided a group of supernatural tales and traditions concerning Alloway Kirk, which then featured in Francis's book.

[24] Ibid., Vol. X, p. 26.

These anecdotes took Burns back to his childhood and lost influences. They also triggered a major literary production in a period when Robert was divided between collecting songs and fulfilling his exhausting duties as an Excise Officer.

'Tam O' Shanter' has a compelling narrative opening that reprises the storyteller's art, which is implicit in many of Burns's early poems but not fully exploited until this juncture in 1791.

When chapman billies leave the street,	pedlar fellows
And drouthy neebors, neebors meet,	thirsty neighbours
As market-days are wearing late,	
An' folk begin to tak the gate;	head home
While we sit bousing at the nappy,	boozing / ale
And getting fou and unco happy,	drunk / very
We think na on the lang Scots miles,	long
The mosses, waters, slaps, and styles,	gaps
That lie between us and our hame,	home
Where sits our sulky sullen dame,	
Gathering her brows like gathering storm,	
Nursing her wrath to keep it warm.[25]	

From the start, however, Burns signals that this will be no naïve reversion to childhood folktales. The quotation at the head of the text is from Gavin Douglas's sixteenth-century translation of Virgil's *Aeneid*: 'Of Brownyis and of Bogillis full is this Buke.' In claiming a succession from Virgil to the sixteenth-century Scots makars, and then to himself, Burns

[25] Ibid., Vol. II, p. 207.

has part of his tongue in his cheek, but only part. 'Honest Tam' is a mock-heroic substitute for Virgil's 'Pious Aeneas' on his perilous journey. The narrator remains finely balanced between sympathy and ironic detachment throughout.

Tam's travels begin from his own personal Eden, the fellowship of the tavern. Here, despite his wife Kate's dire prognostications, Tam is at ease with himself and the world.

Ae market-night,	one
Tam had got planted unco right;	just / especially
Fast by an ingle, bleezing finely,	
Wi' reaming swats that drank divinely	foaming fresh ale
And at his elbow Souter Johnie,	Cobbler
His ancient, trusty, drouthy crony;	
Tam lo'ed him like a very brither –	loved / brother
They had been fou for weeks thegither!	together
The night drave on wi' sangs and clatter	drove / songs
And ay the ale was growing better:	
The landlady and Tam grew gracious,	
Wi' favours, secret, sweet and precious:	
The Souter tauld his queerest stories;	told
The landlord's laugh was ready chorus:	
The storm without might rair and rustle,	roar
Tam didna mind the storm a whistle.[26]	

Good company, friendship, a drink and cultural entertainment have combined to cheat time and care.

[26] Ibid., Vol. II, p. 209.

But pleasures are like poppies spread,
You seize the flower, its bloom is shed;
Or like the snow falls in the river,
A moment white – then melts for ever;
Or like the borealis race,
That flit ere you can point their place;
Or like the rainbow's lovely form
Evanishing amid the storm. –
Nae man can tether time or tide;   no
The hour approaches Tam maun ride;   must
That hour, o' night's black arch the key-stane,
That dreary hour he mounts his beast in;
And sic a night he taks the road in,
As ne'er poor sinner was abroad in.[27]

Around this scene of domestic good cheer, storm clouds are gathering: 'That night a child might understand / The deil had business on his hand.' But Tam is too caught up in his own pleasures to notice. Yet, the story cannot have it any other way. Would we prefer him to linger at the inn or, even worse, to have stayed at home in the first place?

Tam sets out on his inevitable journey because the convivial tavern is not, in reality, home. And home is some miles distant through the storm. As he rides out, Tam has two consolations – his 'guid mare Meg' and the auld Scots sonnets which he croons. The modern Scottish poet, Kenneth White, has pointed out the connection between 'Tam O' Shanter' and 'Tam the Chanter'. Tam is himself a poet and singer with the

[27] Ibid., Vol. II, p. 210.

inspiration of Scots tradition at his disposal. This perspective qualifies and expands the notion of Tam as a sociable drunk. In reality, he is inspired by music, stories, poetry, songs and alcohol, rather like his creator Robert Burns.

Tam's ongoing journey is a rehearsal of popular story-telling tradition and its intimate connection with a living landscape.

By this time he was cross the ford,	
Whare in the snaw the chapman smoor'd:	snow / smothered
And past the birks and meikle stane,	big stone
Whare drunken Charlie brak's neck-bane;	broke his
And thro' the whins, and by the cairn,	
Whare hunters fand the murder'd bairn;	found
And near the thorn, aboon the well,	above
Whare Mungo's mither hang'd hersel. –	mother
Before him Doon pours all his floods;	
The doubling storm roars thro' the woods;	
The lightnings flash from pole to pole;	
Near and more near the thunders roll:	
When, glimmering thro' the groaning trees,	
Kirk-Alloway seemed in a bleeze;	blaze
Thro' ilka bore the beams were glancing;	every hole
And loud resounded mirth and dancing.[28]	

This passage puts to rest Ted Cowan's worries that Burns did not sufficiently value the culture of the people. At Alloway Kirk Tam encounters a folk festivity at full throttle.

[28] Ibid., Vol. II, pp. 211–12.

And, vow! Tam saw an unco sight!	strange
Warlocks and witches in a dance;	
Nae cotillion brent new frae France,	brought
But hornpipes, jigs, strathspeys, and reels,	
Put life and mettle in their heels.	
A winnock-bunker in the east,	window recess
There sat auld Nick, in shape o' beast;	old
A tousie tyke, black, grim and large,	shaggy dog
To gie them music was his charge:	give
He screw'd the pipes and gart them skirl,	made them scream
Till roof and rafters a' did dirl!	vibrate
Coffins stood round like open presses,	cupboards
That shaw'd the dead in their last dresses;	
And by some devilish cantraip sleight,	weird trick
Each in its cauld hand held a light.[29]	cold

This description has a long series of literary ancestors from medieval Scots poetry through to Robert Fergusson and Burns's own 'The Holy Fair'. But Burns's surreal masterstroke is to rewrite the folk tradition with a witches' Sabbath presided over by the Devil himself. Only, in this case, 'Auld Nick' is a bagpiper providing musical overdrive for the dance and even raising the coffin lids. All of life and death is in the spectacle before Tam's eyes, from the gory relics of murder laid out on the sacrilegious Communion Table to the sexual energy of the central character, Nannie, in her cutty sark or mini nightshirt. It is one hell of a party.

[29] Ibid., Vol. II, pp. 212–13.

There is nothing here in essence that Burns has not already seen at Poosie Nancy's, and celebrated in his 'Love and Liberty' hymn to the life energies of drink, sex and social abandon. But 'Tam O' Shanter' raises the game by drawing in religion and bringing the undercover antics of 'The Holy Fair' to a riotously explicit climax. 'Nannie' is the embodiment of pure sexual energy and a force of life that sweeps aside everything in its path with destructive wilfulness. She is the *femme fatale* unleashed.

But Tam kend what was what fu' brawlie,	knew / full well
There was ae winsome wench and wawlie,	choice
That night enlisted in the core,	
(Lang after kend on Carrick shore;	
for mony a beast to dead the shot,	many
An' perish'd mony a bonie boat,	
And shook baith meikle corn and bear,	both much / barley
And kept the country-side in fear).[30]	

Before such a display even poetry must withdraw, and Tam loses self-control.

But here my Muse her wing maun cour;	must curb
Sic flights are far beyond her pow'r;	
To sing how Nannie lap and flang,	leapt and flung
(A souple jade she was, and strang),	supple
And how Tam stood like ane bewitch'd,	one
And thought his very een enriche'd;	eyes
Even Satan glowr'd, and fidg'd fu' fain,	fidgeted eagerly

[30] Ibid., Vol. II, pp. 214–15.

And hotch'd and blew wi' might and main:	jerked
Till first ae caper, syne anither,	one / then another
Tam tint his reason a' thegither,	lost / all togehter
And roars out, 'Weel done, Cutty-sark!'	well done short shirt
And in an instant all was dark;	
And scarcely had he Maggie rallied,	
When out the hellish legion sallied.[31]	

Tam is an outsider to this scene like the poet of 'Love and Liberty'. But the involuntary cry of 'Weel done, Cutty-sark' crosses the boundary between appreciating and contributing. It is an act of folly which exposes Tam's behaviour up to this critical point as an accumulation of folly. By intervening in a rude and uninvited fashion, Tam unleashes demonic forces. Involuntary intrusion on a supernatural scene, resulting in a furious backlash, is a classic folktale motif, but here it has an artistic analogue: when the poet joins the orgy he ceases to be a poet. Yet, as a human being, Tam's desires are aroused and he wants to join the dance.

Tam escapes due to the wit of Maggie, the horse, whose unbefuddled animal instincts have, throughout, been wiser than Tam's inspirations. There is, however, a price to be paid. As the 'fairy host' pursue Tam, Maggie carries him over 'a running stream', which is sure protection against this supernatural danger but, in the process, she loses her tail to the witches.

For Nannie, far before the rest,
Hard upon noble Maggie prest,

[31] Ibid., Vol. II, pp. 215–16.

And flew at Tam wi' furious ettle;	aim
But little wist she Maggie's mettle –	was
Ae spring brought off her master hale,	one
But left behind her ain grey tail:	own
The carlin caught her by the rump,	witch
And left poor Maggie scarce a stump.[32]	

Tam has to return to the domestic hearth a saddened, chastened and reduced man. Art and drink combined have pushed him over a dangerous edge from which he has been retrieved at significant cost to his own life energies, as represented by the faithful and now docked mare, Meg. The nagging wife Kate will be triumphant and in future control of wandering Tam. He has neither played safe nor consummated his moment of ecstasy.

O Tam, had'st thou but been sae wise	
As taen thy ain wife Kate's advice!	taken
She tauld thee weel thou was a skellum,	rogue
A blethering, blustering, drunken blellum,	blabber
That frae November till October,	
Ae market-day thou was nae sober;	not
That ilka melder, wi' the miller,	every grinding
Thou sat as lang as thou had siller;	long / money
That ev'ry naig was ca'd a shoe on,	nag / shot
The smith and thee gat roaring fou on,	
That at the Lord's house, even on Sunday,	
Thou drank wi' Kirkton Jean till Monday.	
She prophesied that late or soon,	

32 Ibid., Vol. II, p. 217.

Thou would be found deep drown'd in Doon;   River Don
Or catch'd wi' warlocks in the mirk,   dark
By Alloway's auld, haunted kirk.[33]   old

'Tam O' Shanter' encapsulates the tension between Burns's folk culture and his Enlightenment convictions. It is also an artistic confession of conflict between instinctive life energies and the demands of art. Tam is a mock hero, but a hero nonetheless, and an ironic alter ego for the poet. Having descended into a dark night of chaos, the hero does not achieve a complete surrender of self or resurrection and rebirth. Burns as artist and thinker is not willing to yield reason and emotion to pure instinct, yet instinctively feels that something has been lost in the process. The energy and abandon of Folly is experienced but rejected in favour of Wisdom, with a rueful sense of life passing by. For Burns, self-mastery remains the highest goal, even when honoured more 'in the breach than in the observing'.

That is why 'Tam O' Shanter' strikes an elegiac note amid the mock-heroic fireworks – 'But pleasures are like poppies spread / You seize the flower its bloom is shed'. This note is taken up in a series of poems provided to William Creech for a second *Edinburgh Edition* of Burns's poems in 1793. The new works begin with lines 'Written in Friar's Carse Hermitage', a reflective retreat provided for the poet by his landed neighbour, Robert Riddell.

Thou whom chance may hither lead,
Be thou clad in russet weed,

[33] Ibid., Vol. II, p. 208.

Be thou deckt in silken stole,
Grave these counsels on thy soul.

Life is but a day at most,
Sprung from night, in darkness lost:
Hope not sunshine ev'ry hour,
Fear not clouds will always lour.[34]

The mood here is of passion spent and, to some degree, regretted. The lessons to be drawn and passed on to a younger generation are intensely moral.

As the shades of ev'ning close,
Beck'ning thee to long repose;
As life itself becomes disease,
Seek the chimney-nook of Ease.
There ruminate with sober thought;
On all thou'st seen, and heard, and wrought;
And teach the sportive younkers round,
Saws of experience, sage and sound:
Say, man's true, genuine estimate,
The grand criterion of his fate,
Is not, Art thou high or low?
Did thy fortune ebb or flow?
Did many talents gild thy span?
Or frugal Nature grudge thee one?
Tell them, and press it on their mind,
As thou thyself must shortly find,
The smile or frown of awful Heav'n,

[34] Ibid., Vol. II, p. 171.

To Virtue or to Vice is giv'n;
Say, to be just, and kind, and wise –
There solid self-enjoyment lies;
That foolish, selfish, faithless ways
Lead to be wretched, vile, and base.[35]

The determinedly resigned tone of these lines is qualified, to a degree, by their being ascribed to 'the Beadsman of Nithside' rather than the poet's own voice. But variations on the theme continue with a vigorous life-affirming elegy to Burns's Edinburgh friend, Matthew Henderson, and a historic 'Lament of Mary Queen of Scots', partly written for Robert Riddell's sister-in-law Maria. The Henderson elegy is an underestimated and little-known poem which pitches the admirable, yet unrecognised, qualities of the deceased against the auld enemy.

O Death! thou tyrant fell and bloody!	
The meikle Devil wi' a woodie	big / halter
Haurl thee hame to his black smiddie,	drag / home / smithy
O'er hurcheon hides,	hedgehog
And like stock-fish come o'er his studdie	anvil
Wi' thy auld sides!	
He's gane! he's gane! he's frae us torn,	gone
The ae best fellow e'er was born!	one / ever
Thee, Matthew, Nature's sel' shall mourn	self
By wood and wild,	

[35] Ibid., Vol. II, pp. 172–3.

Where, haply, Pity strays forlorn
            Frae man exil'd.[36]

In an extended and magnificently realised conceit, the poet
calls on every facet of nature to mourn their loss. Compared
to the laboured Dundas elegy this is gold to dross, and Burns
defiantly affirms the contrast.

Oh Henderson! the man! the brother!
And art thou gone, and gone for ever?
And hast thou crost that unknown river,
            Life's dreary bound?
Like thee, where shall I find another
            The world around?

Go to your sculptur'd tombs, ye Great,
In a' the tinsel trash o' state!
But by thy honest turf I'll wait,
            Thou man of worth!
And weep the ae best fellow's fate
            E'er lay in earth.[37]

In his 'Lament of Mary' Burns again yields to a dramatic
persona, that of the imprisoned Queen. In the tradition of
the medieval makers, the poet looks to the natural world
to resonate with the human condition, but in vain, since
even the simplest forms of life enjoy a freedom denied the
Sovereign.

[36] Ibid., Vol. II, p. 183.
[37] Ibid., Vol. II, pp. 183–4.

Now Nature hangs her mantle green
  On every blooming tree,
And spreads her sheets o' daisies white
  Out o'er the grassy lea:
Now Phoebus cheers the crystal streams,
  And glads the azure skies;
But nought can glad the weary wight
  That fast in durance lies.

Now laverocks wake the merry morn,   larks
  Aloft on dewy wing;
The merle, in his noontide bow'r,   blackbird
  Makes woodland echoes ring;
The mavis wild wi' monie a note,   thrush / many
  Sings drowsy day to rest:
In love and freedom they rejoice,
  Wi' care nor thrall opprest.

Now blooms the lily by the bank,
  The primrose down the brae;   hillside
The hawthorn's budding in the glen,
  And milk-white is the slae: sloe
The meanest hind in fair Scotland
  May rove their sweets amang;   among
But I, the Queen of a' Scotland,
  Maun lie in prison strang![38]   must / strong

The 'Lament' is another fine artistic achievement but also
a further exploration of the tensions between freedom and

[38] Ibid., Vol. II, pp. 187–8.

constraint. For Mary there is neither release nor resolution this side of the grave.

O soon, to me, may Summer suns
    Nae mair light up the morn!   no more
Nae mair, to me, the Autumn winds
    Wave o'er the yellow corn!
And in the narrow house o' death
    Let Winter round me rave;
And the next flowers, that deck the Spring,
    Bloom on my peaceful grave.[39]

In the last few years of his foreshortened life, the passing of time and the prospect of death preoccupy Burns's poetry, outwith the songs of political protest. Yet the mood is never bitter or resentful. The fragility of life calls forth sympathy and sensitivity rather than anger or defiance. Many of these late poems have a spontaneous quality – the feel of immediate response to personal circumstances – and together they constitute an artistic achievement unequalled in Burns's oeuvre. Still only in his late thirties, Robert was producing new work of outstanding freshness, combining technical virtuosity with assured simplicity. The leitmotiv is compassionate wisdom as, for Burns, any sense of immortality is rooted in the values of this mortal existence, raised to a higher purer pitch of perception.

First among these poems is the tender 'On the Birth of a Posthumous Child', written for Mrs Dunlop's daughter, Susan, following the untimely death of her French husband.

[39] Ibid., Vol. II, p. 189.

Sweet flow'ret, pledge o' meikle love,   much
And ward o' monie a prayer,   many
What heart o' stane wad thou na move,   stone would not
Sae helpless, sweet, and fair!

November hirples o'er the lea,   limps
Chill, on thy lovely form;
And gane, alas! the shelt'ring tree,   gone
Should shield thee frae the storm.   from

May He who gives the rain to pour,
And wings the blast to blaw,
Protect thee frae the driving show'r,
The bitter frost and snaw!   snow

May He, the friend of Woe and Want,
Who heals life's various stounds,
Protect and guard the mother plant,
And heal her cruel wounds![40]

Despite the sad circumstances of the birth, it is still a sign of life and renewal and, as Burns's own health woes multiplied, his appreciation of living beauty became even more intense and exquisite. But so did his sense of the imperative to respect and cherish life despite worldly prudence and social constraint. 'O Poortith Cauld' was placed in the mouth of a poor yet sincere lover rejected in favour of a wordly success.

O Poortith cauld and restless love,   cold Poverty
Ye wrack my peace between ye!

[40] Ibid., Vol. II, pp. 243–4.

Yet poortith a' I could forgive
          An 'twere na for my Jeanie.   it were not

Oh why should Fate sic pleasure have,
          Life's dearest bands untwining?
Or why sae sweet a flower as love
          Depend on Fortune's shining?

The warld's wealth when I think on,   world's
          Its pride and a' the lave o't –   rest of it
My curse on silly coward man,
          That he should be the slave o't![41]

According to the rejected lover, the 'wild-wood Indian's fate', released from considerations of wealth and power, is blessed compared to his situation.

During Robert's last extended illness, a young neighbour, Jessie Lewars, came to help Jean as she struggled to cope with a sick husband and a growing family. Jessie inspired two fine song poems, the first a testament to love's vitality, even in the face of death.

O were my love yon lilack fair
          Wi' purple blossoms to the spring,
And I, a bird to shelter there,
          When wearied on my little wing,
How I wad mourn when it was torn
          By Autumn wild and winter rude!

41 Ibid., Vol. V, pp. 97–8.

But I wad sing on wanton wing,   would
      When youthfu' May its bloom renew'd.[42]

The second is an evocation of compassionate love, inspired
by the beauty and fragility of life as embodied by Jessie.

Oh wert thou in the cauld blast,   were / cold
      On yonder lea, on yonder lea;
My plaidie to the angry airt,   plaid / direction
      I'd shelter thee, I'd shelter thee:
Or did Misfortune's bitter storms
      Around thee blaw, around thee blaw   blow
Thy bield should be my bosom,   shelter
      To share it a', to share it a'.[43]

However, the finest blend of poetic creation and traditional
song which Burns achieved in this late phase is surely written
with Jean Armour in mind. 'Auld Lang Syne' is a hymn to
memory and to young love, yet paradoxically it is also an
act of anticipation, forecasting a time or condition which
Burns and his faithful loving wife were not destined to reach.
Nonetheless, the companionship evoked here is a realised,
rather than an anticipated, emotion.

Should auld acquaintance be forgot   old
      And never brought to mind?
Should auld acquaintance be forgot,
      And auld lang syne!   days long since

[42] Ibid., Vol. V, pp. 198–9.
[43] Ibid., Vol. V, p. 282.

And surely ye'll be your pint stowp,   tankard
        And surely I'll be mine,
And we'll tak a cup o' kindness yet,
        For auld lang syne!

We twa hae run about the braes,   two / hillsides
        And pou'd the gowans fine;   pulled
But we've wandered mony a weary fit,   many
        Sin auld lang syne.   since

We two hae paidl'd in the burn,   paddled
        Frae morning sun till dine,   from / dinnertime
But seas between us braid hae roar'd   broad have
        Sin auld lang syne.[44]

Characteristically for Burns, friendship and love are celebrated as social bonds which extend to a universal human fellowship sealed in a loving cup.

And here's a hand, my trusty fiere,   friend
        And gie's a hand o' thine,   give me
And we'll tak a right gude-willie waught,   goodwill draught
        For auld lang syne![45]

The continued popularity of the song is the finest tribute Robert could have desired as man and poet.

[44] Ibid., Vol. IV, pp. 343–4.
[45] Ibid., Vol. IV, pp. 344–5.

Chapter Seven

Laying the Turf

As a man and poet Robert Burns was distinctively of his time and place. Yet his legacy has been claimed by nearly every strand of modern Scottish life.

Liberal Presbyterianism, despite residual carping, has honoured the poet with a huge memorial window in St Giles Cathedral, dwarfing anything offered to other literary figures, or even John Knox. Yet Burns is also a humanist icon, celebrated by the contemporary Scottish literary renaissance.

On the political front, Burns is heralded as the patron saint of democracy while socialists, communists and nationalists energetically claim him for their own. Successive openings of the restored Scottish Parliament have found their intellectual and emotional centres of gravity in 'A Man's a Man For a' That' and 'Auld Lang Syne'.

In cultural terms, Burns is hailed as the embodiment of Scottishness and internationalism. He is radical still in his art and in his challenge to an unjust world order. But Burns is also radical in his comprehensive religious vision, which exposes the prevailing materialist presumptions of his time and ours as hollow, life-denying and destructive. That vision counteracts the complacent mediocrity of present-day managerialism, while vividly reminding us of the beauty and the sadness of nature, the folly and the wisdom of humankind, the possibilities of God.

Burns restores to us the purpose of literature, and recovers what it means to be fully human in a contradictory world. Neither in life nor art is the poet a model of perfection, but that brings him closer to people. His frustration, hardships and faith are something everyone can understand and share.

Further Reading

Alan Bold, *The Burns Companion* (London: Macmillan, 1991)

Thomas Crawford, *Burns: A Study of the Poems and Songs* (Edinburgh: James Thin, 1978)

James Kinsley (ed.), *The Poems and Songs of Robert Burns* (Oxford: Oxford University Press, 1968), three volumes

Donald A. Low (ed.), *Critical Essays on Robert Burns* (London: Routledge & Kegan Paul, 1975)

Donald A. Low (ed.), *Robert Burns: The Critical Heritage* (London: Routledge & Kegan Paul, 1974)

J. Walter McGinty, *Robert Burns and Religion* (Aldershot: Ashgate Publishing, 2003)

Liam McIlvanney, *Burns the Radical: Poetry and Politics in Late Eighteenth Century Scotland* (East Linton: Tuckwell Press, 2002)

Ian McIntyre, *Dirt & Deity: A Life of Robert Burns* (London: Harper Collins, 1995)

James Mackay, *Burns: A Biography of Robert Burns* (Edinburgh: Mainstream Publishing, 1992)

John MacQueen, *Progress and Poetry: The Enlightenment and Scottish Literature* (Edinburgh: Scottish Academic Press, 1982)

Andrew Noble and Patrick Scott Hogg (eds), *The Canongate Burns* (Edinburgh: Canongate Classics, 2001)

Kenneth Simpson (ed.), *Burns Now* (Edinburgh: Canongate, 1994)

Kenneth Simpson (ed.), *Love and Liberty: Robert Burns, A Bicentenary Celebration* (East Lothian: Tuckwell Press, 1997)

Gavin Sprott, *Robert Burns: Pride and Passion* (Edinburgh: HMSO, 1996)

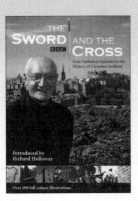

Mr Hill's Big Picture

The Day that Changed Scotland Forever
– Captured on Canvas

By JOHN FOWLER

£8.99 ❖ 978–0–7152–0823–6 ❖ Paperback

In 1843, the great Disruption in the Church divided society in Scotland sharply, embittering relationships and creating long-lasting hostility. The artist David Octavius Hill, with the help of a talented early photographer, captured this decisive moment on an incredible canvas – rarely has a painting so successfully portrayed in such detail such momentous events. This is the story of that painting and the events that inspired it.

SAINT ANDREW PRESS